The Works Of Voltaire

To
E. R. Duckworth
his sketch of Voltaire: by Nino H. P...
Abul. 1903

INDEX

WORKS, GENIU... AND ...

APPRECI...

BY

OLIVER ...

THE WERNER COMPANY
1895

VOLTAIRE, F.

INDEX

TO HIS

WORKS, GENIUS, AND CHARACTER

WITH AN

APPRECIATION

OF VOLTAIRE

BY

OLIVER H. G. LEIGH

AND A PORTRAIT STUDY
IN PHOTOGRAVURE

"He goes to the bottom of every subject, while he only seems to skim the surface."

AKRON, OHIO
THE WERNER COMPANY
1905

Copyright 1903

BY

E. R. DuMONT.

Voltatre Index.

Owned by
The Werner Company
Akron, Ohio

Made by
The Werner Company
Akron, Ohio

THE VOLTAIRE PORTRAIT

This sketch is an attempt to realize the dignity of character that must always have given unusual impressiveness to a face so lit up with French vivacity. The few portraits that have come down to us are the work of artists who were chiefly attracted by Voltaire's brilliance. The admirable bust by Houdon (who was brought to this country to take a life-mask of Washington for the national statue), depicts the keen critic and satirist rather than the student and philosopher. Its smirk and gesture, its theatrical air, convey little or no suggestion of the philanthropist, the life-long champion of the persecuted, the author of the epoch-making "Treatise on Toleration."

Huber's miniature outline sketches cleverly portray the wonderfully expressive face in a number of character and caricature types, with a success few actors can hope to approach. The portraits of Voltaire as a young man and in mid-age are only conventional, and even the later ones, when time and ripe genius had graven those eloquent lines that give such power to a naturally fascinating countenance, are rendered tame by the absurd wigs and frills that have robbed us of the veritable likenesses of so many famous men.

This, then, is an honest attempt to reproduce the lineaments of Voltaire from the several accurate, but single-mood, portraits. It seeks to combine the lighter characteristics of the many-sided and gifted wit and philosopher with those profounder qualities of heart and brain, showing him in his mellow years, the champion of right victorious, and the pioneer of our century's enlightened thought, a noble face that would have given distinction to any equally gifted wearer of the Papal tiara.

O. H. G. L.

50

VOLTAIRE

AN APPRECIATION OF HIS

CHARACTER : GENIUS : WORKS

BY OLIVER H. G. LEIGH

Custom dulls our perceptions of the ludicrous, as the conventionalities of our familiar speech and manners prove. It is responsible for graver offenses than that of enslaving us to harmless absurdities. It has lent a make-believe verity to many a deep-rooted delusion, and fixed rose-tinted spectacles on eyes that have never since tried to see the truth in plain daylight. Most of us whose mother tongue is English were brought up in the vague belief that Cowper's "brilliant Frenchman," Voltaire, was an atheist. In our mildest moods he was at best an "infidel." Pious custom, well-meaning in its good old grandmotherly way, deemed it right and wise to administer this sort of soporific so liberally that the average lifetime might glide away without our awakening sufficiently to see that the only "infidels" are those who, professing a belief, become secretly unfaithful to it. This absurd, or heinous, infidelity is more apparent in those who wear the livery and accept the wages of an established profession, whose instructions they evade or defy, yet do not resign.

To this powerful source we owe tne curious fact that four generations of enlightened American and British people have grown up in less pardonable ignorance than that of Christianized heathen tribes, respecting the character and motives, the philosophical, philanthropic, and literary life-work of Voltaire. Strange indeed that the vast power of the Church in its myriad manifestations should have spent itself these hundred and fifty years in showing bitter intolerance, and inspiring its very children with intolerance, against the greatest Apostle of Toleration known to these generations, the like of whom the Church cannot point to within its pale, unless it rashly names that universally revered Martyr to churchly intolerance, who neither founded, nor drew up a creed for, the once despotic organization that used His name as its phylactery.

Champions and martyrs have never been lacking on the side of intellectual liberty against dogmatic theology and its resultant intolerance of free thinking and plain speaking. But the philosophic temper is averse to the fighting methods which delight the multitude. It views with smiling disdain the encounters between belligerents ill equipped with the kind of weapons that strike deep and deal mortal blows unperceived by the spectators. Perhaps the scholar has not even yet received his due for the quiet but tremendous upheaval he has wrought in the siege of the mediæval fortress of ignorance. Erasmus is even yet virtually unknown to those who all but deify his boisterous out-door workman, Luther.

There has been no champion but Voltaire who has combined the qualities of the philosopher with those of the agile master of the fencing art, who has played so lightly around his adversary while serving such subtle thrusts as are possible only to men of the profoundest learning. He is a phenomenon among ordinary mortals in the variety and solidity of his gifts and accomplishments, but more conspicuously so in this—that a man so overwhelmed with the honors, the rewards, the intoxicating delights of the gay world in which empresses, kings, the famous men of Europe, were his flattering friends, and the people of Paris, adorers of his wit and dramas, should at the same time be the most powerful advocate of the rights of the weak poor against oppressive kings and prelates.

This amazing duality of character is matched by the versatility of resources which enabled him at any moment to cross swords with a dozen opponents, coming at him from different points with different weapons, and to leave them floundering.

Before examining the evidence it is well to trace the influences that developed Voltaire's character. Chief among these influences was the nearly three years' visit he paid to England. Intolerance it was that caused that fortunate experience. He had been consigned to the Bastille a second time, and was freed on his promise of self-expatriation. Voltaire must himself be consulted to get a full understanding of the impression made on him by the sight of a people happy under laws which secured them liberty of religion, of thought, and speech. Less liberty than we are supposed to enjoy to-day, no doubt, but perhaps as much as they could safely stand in those days, and at any rate beyond the dreams of the French.

In Volume XXXIX, and frequently through the others, Voltaire shows that he had seen a great light, and having kindled his torch he was resolved to spread it in his own darker land. His character-istic thoroughness is to the fore here as everywhere. So famous was his name, even in a country bigoted against everything French, that, though not yet thirty-three, he was enthusiastically welcomed by the intellectual ranks. We can hardly realize the weight of England's tribute to Voltaire's genius and char-acter implied in the bare statement that he won the friendship of Alexander Pope, a Catholic; Dean Swift; Young, the poet; Lord Chesterfield; the Duchess of Marlborough; James Thomson, the poet; Lord Bolingbroke, Oliver Goldsmith, Gay, Bubb Dodington, Congreve, Sir Everard Falkener, and many equally gifted. These names stand for social eminence, and much more than that. Sir Isaac Newton had Voltaire as a true mourner at his funeral, and as a life-long disciple who translated and expounded the Newtonian philosophy for the French, and to him the English owe the story of the falling apple that started Newton on his famous discovery. Voltaire was elected a Fellow of the Royal Society for the Advancement of Science, the highest honor of its kind then and now, conferred for substantial service.

This experience was the turning point of his great

career. He had mastered the language, and wrote essays and verses in it, within a year. He absorbed the spirit which, despite a thousand drawbacks, has bred in that people a broader conception of true liberty and has inspired them with a deeper reverence for the laws which secure it than is everywhere to be found. When he returned to France there set a foot on its shore which from that hour knew no rest while a mission of practical sympathy was possible to the oppressed, or an abuse of power could be kicked and trampled down.

Two conspicuous traits of character must impress the most superficial reader. Voltaire was, in literally every sense of a word sadly weakened by daily misuse, a *great* writer, great in depth, force, brilliance, variety, breadth of knowledge, and great too, in quantity. But he was also *great* as a man of affairs, man of the world, the world of Paris and European courts. Something stronger than what we call genius is required to sustain this dual *rôle*. Our geniuses have generally lost in backbone what they gained in their brainpans. Voltaire undoubtedly excelled in the courtier knack of making profound obeisances to royalties, an accomplishment we of this plainer age view much as we might the fitness of a giant for curtseying to a midget. But the backbone was there, ever erect when defiance became its dignity better than pliability, and, for so attenuated a physique, the might of his right arm was astounding to the obese creatures of corruption who reeled under its blows.

Whenever we think of Voltaire as the writer of

the brightest epigrammatic prose, we should remind
ourselves that he is the same man as the pleader
for Toleration, who felt he was criminal if a smile
escaped him during those years of relentless determination to extort public justice and reparation for
the fatal torturing of the innocent Calas. When we
lose ourselves in delight over his piercing raillery of
his dumbstruck priestly victims, we must remember
he is also the grave discourser upon the profundities
of philosophers like Descartes, Newton, Locke, and
the rest as far back as Aristotle and Plato, their
equal in keenness of logic, their superior in giving
it lucid expression. And while we bow our minds
in presence of the Voltaire of the *"Dictionary,"* the
"Essays" and *"Studies,"* let us not forget that it is
the same Voltaire whose tragedies and comedies and
droll tales were the delight of more countries than
his own. And as we pause to realize the full stature
of one whose perfect mental proportions tend to
blind us to the heroic measure of each, we should
make the effort to view him in his workaday clothes,
the shrewd, enterprising business man, who turned
his hand to many undertakings, toiled at them per-
sistently, and prospered as he deserved. All this in
the workshop, the weaving mill, the chemical labora-
tory, the counting room, while part of each day for
sixty years he was also the scholar and teacher, poet
and polemic, in his library; the centre of social
brilliance in the afternoon garden fêtes; the glory
of the dazzling salon in the evenings. Was ever so
thin a mortal compounded of so many distinct indi-
vidualities!

Now let us see some of his achievements. In a day and a continent where industry and trade were regarded with scorn by the aristocracy, Voltaire by his pen and personal example put an end to that suicidal delusion. His letters from England show how strongly he was impressed with her commercial supremacy. He commends her example to his countrymen. Note the pithy literary quality of his short study of this feature [xxxix. 16]. The English alone had passed from feudalism to the stable footing of a commercial nation. Their genius for trade made them great. Their common sense welcomed the younger nobility and men of learned professions in the ranks of trade. How different in Germany and France, says he. "It appears monstrous to a German, whose head is full of the coats of arms and pageants of his family. . . . I have known more than thirty Highnesses of the same name, whose whole fortunes and estate put together amounted to a few coats of arms, and the starving pride they inherited from their ancestors."

Again, coming nearer home: "In France everybody is a marquis; and a man just come from obscurity, with money in his pocket and a name that ends with 'ac' or 'ille' may give himself airs . . . and hold merchants in the most sovereign contempt. . . . I will not, however, take upon me to say which is the most useful to his country, and which of the two ought to have the preference; whether the powdered lord, who knows to a minute when the king rises or goes to bed, perhaps to the bathroom, and who gives himself airs of importance in playing the part of a slave in the ante-chamber of some minister; or the merchant, who enriches his country, and from his counting house sends his orders into Surat or Cairo, thereby contributing to the happiness and convenience of human nature." Voltaire was a benefactor to his country in sound teachings upon practical subjects. Now that merchants are revelling in the zenith of power they may profitably ponder upon the stagnancy from which he aroused his people by his vindication of the dignity of commerce. By a happy balance of favors Voltaire it was who introduced the first company of French actors to the English stage.

How much nineteenth century thought owes of its clearness and force to Voltaire's eighteenth century labors, can hardly be estimated, and can never be over-estimated. The "Higher criticism," of which we hear so much that means so little, stoops lower than its self-respect should permit in concealing its indebtedness to this pioneer of criticism at its highest, boldest, and deadliest. Voltaire set the pace and quality when prison, ignominious burnings of his work by the hangman, and peril of torture or death were the rewards, rather less alluring than the cushioned professorships and publishers' cheques which now crowd the safe field with mediocrities, where the knight of valor fought alone.

Agnosticism finds its most distinguished ancestor and propagandist in Voltaire. Metaphysical reasoners and philosophic doubters will see their favorite original notions threshed out in the "Dictionary" essays and papers in other volumes. Many

a "brilliant" essayist, novelist, major and minor
poet, in more lands than one, has dug in the Voltaire mine for gems of fancy and phrase, still
recognisable by experts despite the ingenious cutting.
Voltaire was compassionate to quacks of every kind
so long as they were harmless. "The unhappy class
who write in order to live" is one kind. "Can there
be greater quackery than the substitution of words
for things, or a wish to make others believe what
we do not believe ourselves?" This refers to a
class who speak more than they read, and read
more than they reflect.

A word for these times in which we live was
spoken by Voltaire in his Address to the French
Academy on his reception to membership. "When
commerce is in a few hands, some people make
prodigious fortunes while the greater number remain
poor; but when commerce is more widely diffused,
wealth becomes general, and great fortunes rare."
For an unsurpassable example of mingled wit, wisdom, scholarship, and delicious candor in mordant
criticism, read the "Discourse to the Welsh,"
[xxxvii. 89] in which excessive national vanity, in
France and elsewhere, is tickled with a jewelled
rapier.

"Ecclesiastics are not the Church." It was against
this man-made ecclesiasticism, and not against pure
religion, that Voltaire flung his destructive thunder-
bombs. In their impious assumption of Godlike
prerogatives these tonsured mummers vengefully
dubbed him "atheist," as Socrates was branded for
holding to his belief in one supreme deity. As well

might we charge Washington with "atheism."
Bishop White, the Father of the Protestant Epis-
copal Church in America, and Washington's pastor,
testified in writing his doubt whether that noble
man was "a believer in the Christian revelation"
further than being an attendant at services but never
a communicant.   How far from atheism was Voltaire's reverent faith and practice is shown in every
writing and act.   "I repeat my *Pater* and *Credo*
every morning."   "I believe in a general Providence,
which has laid down from all eternity the law which
governs all things, like light from the sun."   "The
eyes have mathematical relations so evident, so
demonstrable, so admirable, with the rays of light;
this mechanism is so divine, that I should be tempted
to take for the delirium of a high fever, the audacity
of denying the final causes of their structure."   The
Fathers of the early church built up the creed bit
by bit [in passing, note that popular knowledge of
Holy Writ as a guide book to heaven has never
grasped it as a whole; it has been a scrap-book of
bits of the Bible only], and laid great stress on its
authenticity, and on the point of faith that the saints
who arose at the death of Jesus, died again to rise
with Him a second time.   "The fact is, [says the
pioneer scholar-critic, and his statement is endorsed
by our foremost orthodox scholars] that no person
heard anything of this creed [as it now runs] for
over three hundred years.   People also say that
Paris was not made in a day, and people are often
right in their proverbs. . . .   All these opinions
are absolutely foreign to morality.   We must be

good men, whether the saints were raised once or twice."

Still, due deference should be paid to authority, especially when it gives ocular demonstration of its superior sources of knowledge. "I have no doubt that Pope Leo I. was accompanied by an angel, armed with a flaming sword, which made the king of the Huns tremble. . . . This miracle is very finely painted in the Vatican, and nothing can be clearer than that it never would have been painted unless it had actually been true."

Immense labor went into the making of his Histories. Considering the period, and the pressure of his many occupations, it is nothing short of marvelous that Voltaire was able to ransack the chronicles of older historians, the traditions that are scattered through general writings, the private memoranda and letters of scholars, not to count the personal interviews in which he extracted so much of fact and valuable side light, for the purpose of making his own records truthful. It is well worth while to turn to the passages in which he distinguishes himself, or, rather, his method and purpose, from those of perfunctory narrators of events. He pitched the keynote from which the ablest historians of our time have taken their own, that of helping the reader to look through the smoke of battles to the fate of the plain people who suffered so grievously by the quarrels of kings.

And what exquisite simplicity marks every page. We may smile at an eighteenth century Frenchman's astonishment at Shakespeare's coarseness, and the interesting criticisms upon his dramatic deficiencies. Even Oliver Goldsmith demolished Hamlet's soliloquy with his logic-chopping axe, a weapon he probably borrowed from Voltaire. The author of *"Mérope"* and *"Zaire"* expressly declares, again and again, his view that, at least in the supreme crises, the language should be of the simplest, as in those moments the briefest ejaculations only are natural. There is force in this, but not enough to move us to wish the lines of Hamlet and Othello were prosy. Spots on the sun do not lessen its glory, and if Voltaire cared not, if he could, to soar with the lark that sings at heaven's gate, he stands firm on the green earth as the clearest expresser of penetrating and luminous thought among writers, and he never speaks but with wisdom higher than knowledge, and with motives whose beneficence surpasses even the sparkle of their expression.

A study of these pages will assist in the pleasing duty of doing tardy justice to one of the world's most gifted and powerful intellects. They shed needed light on a man whose character, genius, and far-reaching work have been obscured, but could never be extinguished by the foes of truth-speaking.

VOLTAIREANA

The following are among the innumerable publications relating to Voltaire which appeared during his life and subsequently.

Voltaire; a biographical critique, by John Morley, author of "Diderot and the Encyclopœdists," etc. 1 vol. 8vo. London, 1872; New York and Chicago, 1902, in connection with this edition.

Life of Voltaire. By James Parton. 2 vols. 8vo. Boston and New York. 1881.

The Centenary of Voltaire, May 30, 1878; Oratorical Festival, President, Victor Hugo. Discourses of MM. E. Spuller, Emile Deschanel, and V. Hugo. 32mo., 96 pages. Paris, 1878.

Centenary of Voltaire. By B. Gastineau, 12mo, 36 pages. Brussels. 1878.

To Voltaire! A Poem on the Occasion of the Centenary of Voltaire. By Ernest Calonne. 8vo, 7 pages. Paris. 1878.

Vive Voltaire! Vive Rousseau! Poem by Attale du Cournan. 16mo, 8 pages. Paris. 1878.

Centenary of Voltaire. Poem. By A. Baumann Lyons. 1878.

Centenary of Voltaire. An Appeal to the Good Sense, to the Honor, and to the Patriotism of Men of All Parties. Nismes. 1878.

Centenary of Voltaire. By Members of the United Workmen of St. Etienne. 16mo, 8 pages. St. Etienne. 1878.

The Centenary of Voltaire, followed by the Soul of France. By A. Marquery. A song. 16mo, 4 pages. Paris. 1878.

The Centenary of Voltaire. 4to, 2 pages. Marseilles, 1878.

19

The Centenary of Voltaire in France. 32mo. Paris. 1878.

Historic Gallery of the Actors in the Company of Voltaire. With portraits on steel. 8vo, 2d edition. Recast and augmented. By E. de Maune. Lyons. 1878.

Voltaire and Rousseau, and the Philosophy of the Eighteenth Century. 1 vol. 12mo. By Henri Martin. Paris. 1878.

Voltaire, his Life, his Works, and the Influence of his Ideas upon Society. 1 vol. 12mo. Paris. 1878.

Voltaire in Exile. His Life and his Work in France and in Foreign Lands, Belgium, Holland, Prussia, England, Switzerland. With Unpublished Letters of Voltaire and Madame du Châtelet. By B. Gastineau. 1 vol. 12mo. Paris. 1878.

A German Tourist at Ferney in 1775. By P. Ristelhuber. 1 vol. 16mo. Paris. 1878.

Voltaire in Prussia. By Albert Thieriot. 12mo. Paris. 1878.

Voltaire and Rousseau. By Eugène Noel. 1 vol. 12mo. Paris. 1878.

Frederic II. and Voltaire. Dedicated to the Centenary Commission. 1 vol. 12mo. Paris. 1878.

Prayers, Sermons, and Religious Thoughts. Translated from the French of Voltaire, by J. E. Johnson, Rector of St. John the Evangelist Church, Philadelphia. 1 vol. 16mo. Philadelphia. 1878.

Letters of Madame du Châtelet. Edited by Eugène Asse. 1 vol. 12mo. Paris. 1878.

The Centenary of Voltaire as Celebrated by the Freemasons in Rome. 8vo, 34 pages. Rome. 1878.

Voltairian Iconography. The History and Description of what was published upon Voltaire by Contemporary Art. By Gustave Desnoiresterres. 4 parts, 8vo. Paris. 1878.

Voltaire and the Church. By the Abbé Moussinot. 1 vol. 12mo. Paris. 1878.

One Hundred and One Anecdotes of Voltaire. 1 vol. 12mo. By Gaston de Genonville. Paris. 1878.

The Good and the Evil which has been said of Voltaire. By Maxime de Cideville. 1 vol. 12mo. Paris. 1878.

To Voltaire, a Sonetto (in Italian), with the Translation of the same in French. By Maron Antonio Canini. 8vo, 7 pages. Paris. 1878.

The True Letters of Voltaire to the Abbé Moussinot. Published for the first time from the Autographs in the Bibliothéque Nationale. By Courtat. 12mo. Paris. 1875.

Life and Times of François-Marie Arouet, calling himself Voltaire. By Francis Espinasse. 8vo, London. 1876.

Voltaire and French Society in the Eighteenth Century. A Biography in eight volumes. 8vo. By Gustave Desnoiresterres. Paris. 1876.

Voltaire and the People of Geneva. By J. Gaberel, former pastor. 12mo. Paris. 1857.

The Philosophy of Voltaire. By Ernest Bersot. 12mo. Paris. 1858.

Jean Calas and His Family. An Historic Study from Original Documents. By Athanase Coquerel, Jun., Pastor of the Reformed Church. 12mo. Paris. 1858.

Voltaire at Ferney. His correspondence with the Duchess of Saxe-Gotha. Collected and edited by MM. Evariste and Bavoux. 8vo. Paris. 1860.

Voltaire and His Schoolmasters. An Episode of Classical Learning in France. By Alexis Pierron. 12mo. Paris. 1867.

The True Voltaire, the Man, and the Thinker. By Edouard de Pomery. A Biography. 8vo. Paris. 1867.

Voltaire. By David Frederic Strauss. 1870.

Voltaire and the French Revolution. By C. Nagel. 8vo, 176 pages. 1839.

The Housekeeping and Finance of Voltaire, with an Introduction upon Court and Drawing-Room Manners in the Eighteenth Century. By Louis Nicolardot. 1 vol. 8vo. Paris. 1854.

The Slipper of Voltaire. A Vaudeville in two Acts. By J. B. Simonnin. Paris. 1836.

Voltaire on a Holiday. A Vaudeville in two Acts. By De Villeneuve and De Livry. Paris. 1836.

A Fugitive at the House of Voltaire. A Vaudeville in one Act. By Saint-Hilaire and Simonnin. Paris. 1836.

Voltaire and Madame de Pompadour. A Comedy in three Acts. By J. B. P. Lafitte and C. Desnoyer. Paris. 1833.

The Youth of Voltaire, or the First Prize. An Historical Comedy in one Act, with Couplets intermixed. By Saint-Hilaire. 18mo, 72 pages. Paris. 1833.

Madame du Châtelet, or No To-Morrow. A Comedy in one Act and in Prose, with Songs intermingled. By Ancelot and Gustave. Paris. 1832.

A Breakfast at Ferney in 1765, or the Widow Calas at the Home of Voltaire. A Dramatic Sketch in one Act and in Verse. By Alexandre Duvoisin-Calas. Gustave. Paris. 1832.

Voltaire among the Capuchins. A Comedy in one Act and in Prose, with Songs. By Dumersan and Dupin. Paris. 1830.

An Epistle to Voltaire in Verse. By Lacroix. Pamphlet, 4 pages. Bordeaux. 1831.

Voltaire at Frankfort. An Anecdotical Comedy in one Act and in Prose, with Songs. By Ourry and Brazier. Paris. 1831.

Examination of the Works of Voltaire considered as Poet, as Prose Writer, as Philosopher. By Linquet. 8vo. Paris. 1827.

An Epistle to Voltaire in verse. By M. J. Chénier. Paris. 1806 and 1826.

Voltaire and a Jesuit. A Dialogue in verse. By Constant Taillard. 32mo, 32 pages. Paris. 1826.

Memoirs relating to Voltaire and his Works. By Longchamp and Wagnière, his Secretaries. Followed by various unpublished Writings of the Marquise du Châtelet, Hénault, Piron, D'Arnaud, Thieriot, and others, all relating to Voltaire. 2 vols. 12mo. Paris. 1826.

The Pastoral Address of Monseigneur the Bishop of
Troyes, upon the Printing of bad books, and particularly upon the Complete Works of Voltaire and Rousseau. Pamphlet, 76 pages. Paris, Lyons, and Tou-
louse. 1821.

Letter from M. Touquet to his grandeur Monseigneur the
Bishop of Troyes, Archbishop elect of Vienna, in
reply to his Pastoral Address against the editions of
the Complete Works of Voltaire and J. J. Rousseau.
Pamphlet, 48 pages. Paris. 1821.

Full Presentation of the Voltaire-Touquet, a Collection of
the Treatises, Sentences, Transactions, Judgments, Decrees, and various Acts relative to that Operation (a
suit between publishers). Quarto, 104 pages. Paris.
1823.

History of the Life and Works of Voltaire, with Estimates
of that celebrated man by various esteemed authors.
By L. Paillet de Warcy. 2 vols. 8vo. Paris. 1824.

The Faithful Catholics to the Bishops and all the Pastors
of the Church of France, on the subject of the new
editions of the works of Voltaire and Rousseau. Pamphlet, 52 pages. Paris. 1821.

Private Life of Voltaire and Madame du Châtelet, during
a Sojourn of six Months at Cirey. By the Author of
the Peruvian Letters (Madame de Grafigny), followed
by Fifty Unpublished Letters in verse and in prose of
Voltaire. 1 vol. 8vo. Paris. 1820.

Literary History of Voltaire, containing his literary and
private Life, Anecdotes, and Successes of each of his
works, with Details of the Honors which he obtained
during his life, and those which were decreed to him at
the Temple of great Men. By the Marquis de Luchet.
6 vols. 8vo. Paris. 1792.

To the Manes of Voltaire, a Poem which received the
prize from the French Academy. By J. F. de La
Harpe. Pamphlet. Paris. 1779.

The Fiftieth Dramatic Anniversary of M. de Voltaire, followed by the Inauguration of his Statue. A Medley

in one act and in prose, with songs and dances. By
Du Coudray. Paris. 1774.

Philosophic Picture of the Mind of Voltaire, to serve as
Supplement to his Works. By the Abbé Sabatier.
8vo. Geneva and Paris. 1771.

A Philosophic Delineation of the Mind of M. de Voltaire,
to serve as a Sequel to his Works, and as Memoirs
for the History of his Life. By De Castres. 8vo.
Geneva and Paris. 1771.

The Political Age of Louis XIV., or Letters of the Vis-
count Bolingbroke upon that subject, together with the
pieces which formed the History of the Age of M. de
Voltaire, and of his quarrels with Messrs. de Maupertuis and de La Beaumelle; followed by the Disgrace
of that famous poet. 12mo, 495 pages. Sieclopolis,
(Frankfort.) 1753.

A Comparison of the four Electras, of Sophocles, of
Euripides, of M. de Crébillon, and of M. de Voltaire.
By Gaillard. 124 pages, 12mo. The Hague. 1750.

A Critical Letter, or Comparison of the three ancient epic
Poems, the Iliad and Odyssey of· Homer, and the
Æneid of Virgil, with the League, or Henry the Great,
of M. de Voltaire. By De Bellechaume. 15 pages,
8vo. Paris. 1724.

The King of Prussia's Criticism on the Henriade of M.
Voltaire. Translated from the original; with a preface
containing a short account of the Disgrace and Retreat of that favorite. London. 1760.

Letter from M. de Voltaire to M. Palissot, with the Reply, on the occasion of the Comedy of the Philosophers.
Paris. 1760.

NOTE ON THE INDEX

At first sight the making of an index appears to be a merely mechanical piece of work. So it often is, but it may be much more than this. By way of illustration it may be permissible to mention an elaborate index made by the present writer for a ten volume historical work, of which the publishers say in their prospectus that its original plan and thoroughness make it "worth in itself many times the cost of the entire series of books." This Voltaire index has also been constructed with the intention of making it interesting and valuable in itself, independently of the volumes to which it is a guide.

The editor of a voluminous author has obviously many advantages over an index-maker not previously familiar with the writings and characteristics of his hero. Mr. Percy Fitzgerald may be quoted on this. In his prefatory note to the index he made for his famous edition of Boswell's Life of Dr. Johnson, he says: "No proper or suffi-"cient index can be made vicariously; it requires a "thorough acquaintance with the book treated, so "as to anticipate by a sort of instinct what topics "the reader would desire to search for. Indexes "are generally too minutely elaborate, too meagre, "or too indefinite."

25

How easy it would have been to have filled two or three volumes with the usual index matter can be seen in the fact that Voltaire's pen was never at rest for sixty-three years, and no writer treated so vast a variety of topics. How difficult it has actually been to make selections that shall be equally fair to author and reader, must be left for the user of this index to discern and appraise.

The aim has been to simplify, and in the readiest way provide clues to the innumerable long and short utterances of Voltaire upon subjects treated from every point of view and in every mood. Recurring as he did to the same topics at different periods, with new side lights from intervening occurrences or continued study, he necessarily covers the same ground, though usually with a different gait. To make an index entry of each of these virtual repetitions would cumber every page and weary the reader. And the multiplication of cross-references is no less an offense to the reader's intelligence. These entries are therefore economized, the main clues being liberally given, leaving the reader the pleasure akin to that of intellectual sport in following the various trails in this and that direction where there seems promise of a "find." He may be quite sure of catching something fully as worthy of his hunt as the particular quarry he started after.

Again, there have been occasions when it would have actually broken the continuity of a subject's treatment if the alphabetical or chronological order had been adhered to. Exceptions are often

more practically valuable than rigidity of rule, and
for the liberties so taken no apologies are offered
except that of common sense.   The reader will
find that his interests have been given precedence
over the fads of pedants.

As Voltaire has for so long been virtually unknown to the public at large, one aim of this index
is to open wide the doors of an armory, whose ar-
ray of weapons includes every kind ever used in
warfare, and every one, small and large, still gleams
with its original brightness, mellowed with the
trophy-marks of the good work it has done. These
simple-looking index items, rightly viewed, are in
one aspect the battle roll of a stupendous, single-
handed, life-long fight by a brave truth-lover
against a Juggernaut truth-crusher; and in another
aspect they form a crown of evergreen laurel
leaves, with which a somewhat forgetful generation
is prone to crown its own brow.

Voltaire is here made to portray himself. This
aims to be an index, through his works, of the
man. For this reason there have been scattered
through the ordinary entries examples of his literary style and play of thought.   Epigrammatic
sentences, passages from essays, dramas, and
poems, give life to the dry bones of index matter
and will prove as readable as many of the antholo-
gies and "elegant extracts" now so popular, with
this distinction, that here we have the utterances
of a plain speaker in the days when plain speech
meant peril of life and liberty. Voltaire's piercing

epigrams earned for him the nowadays rarely attainable honors of imprisonment and exile.

If here and there the index item does not literally correspond with the text it is because the brilliance or pungency of Voltairean French can be more effectively reproduced by a paraphrase or a short cut than in the literal translation, and for this offense the result is pleaded in mitigation. Literary expression has changed, as well as incidentals which make eighteenth century allusions obscure or obsolete, and this is particularly the case in renderings of the old verse. A lenient judgment is anticipated from the Shade of Voltaire, as he recalls his own dicta upon this delicate question, and turns at our suggestion to his own translation of Hamlet's soliloquy.

The key-words to the epigrams are, of course, not Voltaire's. They are chosen sometimes as mere titles, again as side lights, and again as provocatives for deeper thought. It can scarcely be necessary to add that Voltaire is not to be held responsible for all the expressions he puts into the mouths of his dramatic characters.

In the histories of Charles XII. and Louis XIV., being masterworks of the historian, full synopses have been given in the index and shorter entries in the Contents. Where the entries are merely of names and topics, they have been made short for a good reason.

No complex piece of work such as this is can be perfect, and doubtless certain of the omissions and condensations made, always after careful deliberation, will be condemned as defects. The culprit anticipates and accepts all criticism in advance with unaffected humility, having tried to earn the solace of feeling that he, as a long-suffering victim of many brain-wasting indexes, would be grateful to anyone who might do for a voluminous author and his readers what has here been conscientiously attempted as helpful to students of Voltaire.   O. H. G. L.

GENERAL CONTENTS

OF

VOLUMES I—XLI

(For List of Illustrations see p. 59.)

VOL. I.

VOL. II.

VOL. III.

VOL. V.

A PHILOSOPHICAL DICTIONARY. In ten volumes.

(See xxxv. 219-288; xxxviii. 231-262; and the
philosophical "Poems.")

VOL. VI.

PHILOSOPHICAL DICTIONARY, continued.

VOL. VII.

PHILOSOPHICAL DICTIONARY, continued.

VOL. VIII.

VOL. XI.

PHILOSOPHICAL DICTIONARY, continued.

VOL. XII.

PHILOSOPHICAL DICTIONARY, continued.

VOL. XIII.

PHILOSOPHICAL DICTIONARY, continued.

VOL. XIV.

PHILOSOPHICAL DICTIONARY, continued.

VOL. XV.

General Contents

VOL. XXV.

ANCIENT AND MODERN HISTORY, continued.

Germany, 1056, to England, 1400.

VOL. XXVI.

VOL. XXVII.

VOL. XXVIII.

VOL. XXXV.

VOL. XL.

VOL. XLI.

LIST OF ILLUSTRATIONS

IN THE

VOLUMES

VOLTAIRE INDEX

[Consult also the entries under "Philosophical Dictionary," at foot of each letter of the Index.]

A

Æ: ALPHABET; origin of language, v. 5.

ABBEY, ABBOTT; historico-theological exposition, v. 15.

ABD-ER-RAHMAN; overruns France and Spain in the eighth century, xxiv. 182.

A'BECKET, THOMAS, xxv. 50, 1119-1170; a lawyer who became chancellor to Henry II. and afterwards Primate of England and Legate of the Holy See; he asserts the church's power over the civil law, 51; refuses to answer charges so is imprisoned by the bishops and lords; flies to France, returns in 1170 and excommunicates those who had condemned him, 51; the king asks if no one will rid him of the insolent prelate, whereupon A'Becket was murdered at the altar of Canterbury cathedral, 1172. King Henry submits to penance and discipline at the tomb, by command of the Pope, 53; canonized as a saint.

ABELARD AND HELOISE, 1079-1142, xi. 141; and St. Bernard, xxvi. 54.

ABELIANS; nudity their rule in worship, xii. 58.

ABLE, ability, v. 27.

ABORTION, the sonnet of the; a court poem of 1673, xxiii. 172.

ABRAHAM, his age and career, v. 29; his journey to Egypt, 39; his relations with Jehovah, 49; the thrifty man of business, viii. 181.

ABSOLUTION, fees for, in cases of homicide, bigamy, heresy, and permission to read forbidden books, xiii. 136; xiv. 65.

ABUSE, abuse of words, v. 53.

ABYSSINIA, its exploration by Alvarez, xxvii. 189.

ACADEMIES and learned societies; Homer, Michelangelo, Sophocles and Virgil were not academicians, xiii. 228.

ACADEMIE FRANCAISE, suggestions toward its improvement, xiii. 232.

ACCIDENTALS.

> "Upon occasion, time and place,
> Depend your glory or disgrace;
> One day by all you're idolized,
> The next insulted and despised."
>
> —*Epistle XIII.* xxxvi. 213.

ACHMET III., Emperor of the Turks, entertains Charles XII. of Sweden lavishly at Bender, xx. 187.

ACTORS AND CHURCH CENSURES. xxxvii. 240; used to be excommunicated, xiii. 322.

ACTORS BOTH. "Prudes love coxcombs."—*The Prude,* xviii. 179.

ADAM, unknown to his descendants, v. 60; lived nine hundred and thirty years after eating his apple, though "in the day that thou eatest thereof thou shalt surely die," xii. 118; the old theologians in doubt whether Adam had or had not a navel, xli. 176.

ADAMITES, a Christian sect that deprived themselves of clothing in public worship, xii. 58.

ADDISON on literary taste, xiv. 52.

ADORATION OF A GOD preceded all forms of religion, xiv. 83.

ADRIAN I., the first Pope who made himself a prince; in the eighth century, xxiv. 88.

ADRIAN, Pope and the Hincmar case, viii. 65.

ADRIAN IV., Pope, d. 1159; was an English beggar named Nicholas Breakspere, the son of a beggar, xxv. 30.

ADRIAN, Vespasian, Nerva, Titus, Trajan, the Antonines; these Roman Emperors never persecuted the Christians, xxiv. 68.

ADRIENNE LECOUVREUR on the death of, xxxvi. 77.

"ADVENTURE IN INDIA, AN;" see ROMANCES.

AERIAL VOYAGE OF HABAKKUK, 300 miles, suspended by a single hair of his head, xiii. 25.

ÆSOP, otherwise Locman, a Persian, xxiv. 45; xxxv. 282.

sesses three abbeys with extensive territories, and twenty thousand slaves, 131.

ALEXANDER THE GREAT, B. C. 356-323; v. 107.

ALEXANDER VI., Pope, 1431-1503; publicly accused of incest, xxvi. 207; disgraceful nuptial festivities in the Vatican, 208; bargains with Louis XII. of France for a divorce, 210; Louis invades Italy, 211; his conquests, 1499, 212; the villainies of the family of this Pope and Cæsar Borgia, 216; murders, oppressions, cheatings, hypocrisies, 217; his strange death, 221; leaving a more detestable memory than did Nero or Caligula, 222. Note, xli. 102.

ALEXANDER VIII., Pope, 1610-1691; no man in the Middle Ages ever deserved so well of mankind, xxx. 137.

ALEXANDER'S FEAST, by Dryden, a masterpiece of lyric verse, viii. 243.

ALFRED THE GREAT, 849-901. "I do not think that there ever was in the world a man more worthy of the regard of posterity than Alfred the Great, who rescued his bleeding country from slavery, and governed her like a good king."   —General History, xxiv. 176.

ALLUREMENT.   "I must cover
The pit with flowers, if I would draw them to it."
                              —Cæsar, xix. 109.

ALONE.
"In this distressful hour the world forsakes me."
                              —Zaïre xix. 59.

ALPHONSO, called the Great, ninth century, King of Spain, who put out the eyes of four of his brothers, xxiv. 185.

ALTENA, the destruction of, Charles XII. of Sweden, xx. 285.

ALTRUISM.
          "What I still would litigate with power,
          I give to friendship; nay, I can do more,
          I can subdue the weakness of my heart,
          And plead a rival's cause."—Amelia, xvi. 91.

principalities, archangels, and angels. It is hardly permissible for anyone but a Pope thus to settle the different ranks in heaven."—v. 202.

ANGER.

"That anger which soon kindled
Is soon extinct, which, doubtful still and blind,
Exhausts its feeble powers in sudden transports."
—*Mariamne*, xvi. 248.

ANIMALIZING. "I have received your new book against the human race. I thank you for it. No one has ever employed so much intellect in the attempt to prove us beasts."   —*Letter* to J. J. Rousseau, xxxviii. 223.

"Annals of the Empire," xxxi-xxxii, continued in xxxiii. Charlemagne, A. D. 742, to Henry VII., 1313, xxxi. 14; Louis of Bavaria, 1315, to Ferdinand II., 1631, xxxii. 5; to Leopold, xxxiii. 259. See Voltaire's Letter to a Professor of History, xxxvii. 280. See Charlemagne, for names of the Emperors.

ANNE, The Heroic Life of St., the Mother of Mary, dictated by Herself to Father Malagrida, xxx. 243.

ANNE, Queen of England, 1664-1714, hated because she had caused peace, xx. 297; xxii. 296.

ANODYNE, THE SLOW.

"Time, my lord,
Will bring back order and tranquillity."
—*Orphan of China*, xv. 211.

ANTHONY OF NAVARRE, father of Henry IV., xxxviii. 27.

ANTICHRIST. "The Jesuit, Molina, 'invented the doctrine of concomitant concurrence, of intermediate knowledge, and congruism.' He was denounced for this as the forerunner of Antichrist." —*Jansenism*, xxi. 144.

ANTIPATHY. "There is no reason why, because we can't love, we should hate each other."
—*Nanine* xviii. 154.

ANTIQUITY, Fables and history in, xxxvii. 257.

ANTI-TOLERATION. *Miscellanies*, xxxviii. 258-260. See Toleration.

ANTS AND BEES, their model governments, xi. 87.

ANVIL, 'TWIXT HAMMER AND. "I fear that in this
world we are reduced to being either the anvil or the
hammer."   —xiv. 135.

APAMIS, Story of, xxxvi. 141.

APING OTHERS. "Apes were made for imitation, but
man should act from his own heart."
                                    —*Nanine*, xxiii. 97.

APOCALYPSE, THE. "The houses in the New Jerusalem of a thousand years were to be five hundred
leagues high. It would be rather disagreeable to live
in the upper story, but we find all this in the twenty-
first chapter."   —v. 245.

APOCRYPHA, New Testament. "St. Clement the Roman
says, in his second Epistle, 'The Lord, being asked when
his reign should come, answered, "When two shall make
one, when that which is without shall be within, when
the male shall be female, and when there shall be
neither female nor male." ' "   —v. 268.

APOSTATE, THE, a vindication of Emperor Julian, xi. 10;
philosopher, statesman, soldier, tolerant as a ruler, 18.

APOSTLES, The, were they married? v. 299.

——Creed, not written by them, vii. 116; how formu-
lated, 118; disputes among the, 138.

APOSTOLICAL CONSTITUTIONS AND CANONS, v. 278.

APOSTOLIC ORIGIN OF THE INQUISITION, x. 218.

APPARITIONS, v. 314; of Jesus in a French church, xiv.
20; of Madame St. Memin, and her extraordinary
news from hell, as reported before a French law
court, xiv. 167.

APPEARANCE, vi. 5.

APPEARANCES MISTAKEN FOR REALITIES, x. 11.

APPEARING AND BEING. "He has a noble heart, and
you may one day know he is not what perhaps he might
appear to be."   —*The Prude*, xviii. 238.

APPRECIATION.

"Presumptuous ignorance long has spurned the head
Of patient merit, which defenceless lay."
                    —*Verses to Frederic of Prussia*, xxxvi. 80.

APRIL SKIES.

> "Nought has earth but shadows vain,
> Of pleasures followed close by pain;
> Soon her winged transports fly,
> Soon her roses fade and die."
>
> —*Pandora*, xvii. 302.

AQUINAS, ST. THOMAS, 1227-1274, "the Eagle of Theology," xxvii. 139.

ARABIA, the genius of its people, its greatness for three
centuries under the Caliphs, xxiv. 60.

ARABIC LANGUAGE. "It was fixed before the time of
Mahomet and has not been altered since, and there is
not the least trace in it of any jargon spoken at that
time in Europe."   —*General History*, xxiv. 65.

ARARAT, MOUNT, on which the Ark rested; story of ship
built by Xixuter on the advice of Saturn, which
weathered the Deluge and was left high and dry on
the top of a mountain in Armenia, vi. 16.

ARBRISSEL, ST. ROBERT, a stronger St. Anthony, xl. 144-
164.

ARCHIMEDES, a problem in love and fate for, ix. 254.

ARIOSTO, viii. 256; forty-eight thousand rhymes without
wearying the reader, xiii. 91; xli. 97.

ARISTEAS, story of Ptolemy Philadelphus, vi. 30.

ARISTOTLE, vi. 33; on eloquence, viii. 199; adored and
cursed by the ignorant men of learning in the church,
xiv. 203.

ARISTOCRACY. "The man of worth, who has modesty
with courage, and the woman who has sense and spirit,
though without fortune, rank, or title, are, in my eyes,
the first of human kind."   —*Nanine*, xviii. 96.

ARIUS, d. 336, his fight with Athanasius, vi. 19.

ARK, NOAH'S, its wonderful capacity, viii. 70. See ARARAT.

ARMADA, the Invincible, of Philip II, 1588, xxviii. 5. See
PHILLIP II.

ARNAULD, disciple of St. Cyran, champion of Jansenism,
xxi. 146-157.

ART AND GENIUS. "Art and genius consist in finding

everything within the subject, and never going out of it in search of additional ornaments."

—Preface to *Orestes*, xvii. 67.

ART AT ITS HIGHEST. "How astonishing it is that in every art it should be so long before we arrive at the simple and natural." —Preface to *Zaïre*, xix. 15.

"ART OF LOVE," the true cause of Ovid's banishment, xii. 129.

ART OF WRITING, Jesus never condescended to practise the, xiv. 104.

ARTAXERXES and the retreat of the ten thousand, an examination of the curious story, xiv. 272.

ARTIFICIAL RELIGION encourages holy wars and atrocities, xiv. 196.

ARTILLERY introduced ten years before the battle of Crécy, in 1346, xxv. 288.

ARTS, the fine, banished from France by the revocation of the Edict of Nantes, vi. 67.

"AS WE FORGIVE OUR DEBTORS." Do we? vi. 270.

ASIA in the thirteenth to the sixteenth centuries, xxvii. 231. See GENGHIS KHAN, CHINA, TAMERLANE.

ASMODEUS, seducer of Eve and Sarah, vi. 72.

ASS OF ANCONA, THE.

"Now, in the pomp of apostolic state,

Supreme, and crowned with empire, (Pope) Sixtus sate;

If fraud and churlish insolence might claim

Renown, no monarch bore a fairer name."

—*The Henriade,* xxxviii. 60.

ASS OF VERONA, THE, which walked on the sea from Jerusalem, xxix. 302.

ASSASSINS. "He who takes

Another's life should lose his own; no rights,

No laws, should plead for him."

—*Catiline* xvii. 274.

—— fortified by receiving the blessed sacrament, xiv. 26; absolution obtainable before perpetration of crimes, xxvii. 301.

ASSES, talking, vi. 81.

"The feast of the Ass of Verona was celebrated in the churches. There was a long procession, headed by a young woman with a child in her arms, mounted on an ass, representing the Virgin Mary going into Egypt. At the end of the mass the priest brayed three times with all his might, and the people answered in chorus."

—vi. 87.

Balaam's ass, xl. 94; xli. 256.

ASSISSI, FRANCIS, xxix. 260; note, xl. 89. See D'ASSISSI.

ASTROLOGY. "This credulity, which is the most infallible mark of ignorance, prevailed so much that an astrologer was kept concealed in the chamber of Queen Anne of Austria, while she was in labor of Louis XIV."

—Age of Louis XIV, xxii. 34.

—— possibly provable, vi. 93; note, xl. 298.

ASTRONOMY, evidence of universal law, vi. 96.

ATHANASIUS, ST., 296-373, his hair-splitting creed, vi. 21.

ATHEISM. "He's a heretic, he denies the plurality of gods! He's a deist; he believes in only one God, he's an atheist!" —Socrates, xvi. 298.

—— unwisdom of, vi. 104; arguments reviewed, philosophy of, 129; xi. 193.

"ATHEIST," Socrates so called because he believed in one God only, xiii. 234.

ATROCITIES of kings and queens in the eighth and ninth centuries, xxiv. 191.

AUGUST CEREMONIES in worship need not involve mysteries, xiii. 63.

AUGUSTINE, saint and man, 354-430, vi. 151; an African debauchee and penitent, Manichœan and Christian, tolerant and persecuting, who passed his life in perpetual self-contradiction, xii. 118; his opinion of St. Paul, vii. 139-157; stories of his miracles, and of St. Jerome, xi. 279; his testimony respecting the custom of having drinking bouts at the tombs of the early Christians, xiii. 57; note, xl. 280, xli. 255.

AUGUSTINE THE MONK, d. 607, who Christianized England, first archbishop of Canterbury, xxiv. 139.

A PHILOSOPHICAL DICTIONARY.

IN TEN VOLUMES—V-XIV.

VOL. V. A TO APPARITION.

kind cutting one another's throats and nothing more."
—*On Printed Lies,* xxi. 281.

BAYARD, CHEVALIER, 1475-1524, the flower of chivalry, xxvii. 17.

BAYLE, PIERRE, 1647-1706, on David the Psalmist, viii. 57; on the philosophy of Ovid, xii. 131; a criticism upon, xxxviii. 271.

BEARD, the impiety of picturing God with a, x. 173; fluctuations of fashion, xxvi. 319.

BEASTS, the souls of, vi. 222.

BEASTS AND MEN. "Dogs bite from an instinct of courage, and this fellow from an instinct of meanness."
—*The Scotch Woman,* xviii. 29.

BEAUMELLE, LAURENT DE LA, note, xl. 218; xli. 185-195.

BEAUTY, when out of its place, is beauty no longer, xiv. 235.

BEAUTY'S FAILINGS. "I would prefer ugliness and affability to beauty with pride and arrogance."
—*Nanine,* xviii. 94.

BEES, contrasted with ourselves, vi. 230.

BEGIN RIGHT. "If you once make yourself ridiculous, in early life, the world will think you always so."
—*The Tatler,* xviii. 263.

BEHEADINGS. "Thoughts on Government," xxxvii. 234.

BELLE-ISLE, Marshal relieves Prague, which was suffering severely, "War of 1741," xxxiii. 90.

BELIEF, believing that we believe, vi. 244.

BELLINI, GENTILE, the painter, 1501, note, xli. 267.

BENEDICT, ST., d. 542, xxvii. 132.

BENEDICTINE MONKS, their services to posterity in raising towns around the monasteries, which were centres of learning and good work among the poor, and a refuge from tyranny, xxiv. 132; note, xl. 119-164.

BENEDICT XIV., Pope, friend of Voltaire, a man of letters and a lover of peace, xxx. 226.

BENEFICENCE towards our neighbor, this is virtue, xiv. 163.

BENEFICENT INVADERS.

> "Conquerors; some were sent by heaven
> To guide our footsteps in the paths of truth,
> To teach us arts unknown, immortal secrets,
> The knowledge of mankind, the arts, my son,
> To speak, to think, to live, and to be happy."
> —*Alsire*, xvii. 25.

BENEFIT OF CLERGY, meaning of term, vii. 197.

BENJAMIN, the tribe almost extirpated by civil war; they kill all the men, married women, and widows, taking six hundred virgins to repair their tribe, xxi. 197.

BENNET, MONASTERY OF ST., where Agnes Sorel was buried, note, xli. 260-262.

BEQUESTS, a kind of Gasconade, xxxvii. 151.

BERKELEY, BISHOP, 1684-1753, his paradoxical doctrine of matter, vi. 261.

BERNARD, ST., 1091-1153, of Clairvaux, v. 18; leader of a Crusade, xxv. 109.

BERNINI, CHEVALIER, Italian architect, employed and honored by Louis XIV., xxiii. 240.

BEROSUS, B. C. 300, the veracious historian and his scholarly fish, x. 145.

BIBLE, history of the Jews, xxi. 193.

BIGOT-BRUTES.

> "See cruel men a burying place refuse
> To her whom Greece had worshipped as a muse;
> When living, they adored her power divine,
> To her they bowed like votaries at a shrine."
> —*Adrienne Lecouvreur*, xxxvi. 77.

BIGOT-HATRED.

> "Prejudice and passion blind thee; I excuse
> Thy weakness, but canst thou hate me?"
> —*Cæsar*, xix. 131.

BIGOT-SLANDER. "But what sort of impiety?" "O, every kind; however, we had best accuse him at once of not believing in the gods; that's the shortest way."
—*Socrates*, xvi. 293.

BIGOT-ZEAL.

> "Wisdom must yield to superstition's rules,
> Who arms with bigot zeal the hands of fools."
>
> —*La Pucelle*, xl. 195.

BIGOTS, PULPITED.

> "He is a wretch indeed who still for pelf
> Damns others, and would almost damn himself."
>
> —*Envy*, xxxvi. 186.

BIOGRAPHICAL ACCOUNT OF VOLTAIRE, i. 15.

BISHOP OF BISCAY, THE, and his heretical ram, ix. 21.

—— portrait of a prelate in fashionable society, vi. 252.

—— Warburton's contention that Job did not believe in immortality, xiii. 282; rise of bishops, xxiv. 129.

BITTERSWEET. "Love is a passion learned with ease."

> —*Pandora*, xvii. 300.

BLACK PRINCE, EDWARD THE, 1330-1376, victor at Crècy and Poitiers, xxv. 288, xxvi. 8, 9, 11, 12.

BLAKE, ADMIRAL, 1598-1657, xxii. 85.

BLANK VERSIFIERS, because they are incapable of rhyme, xiii. 90.

BLASPHEMY, nature and degrees of, vi. 254.

BLASPHEMY, PIOUS.

> "A man does not so much blaspheme,
> Denying God, the judge supreme,
> As when he paints Him to mankind
> As cruel, and to wrath inclined,
> Taking delight in human woes,
> His creatures treating as His foes."
>
> —*Fanaticism*, xxxvi. 271.

BLENHEIM, battle of, xxiii. 30.

BLIND AS JUDGES OF COLOR, THE. See ROMANCES.

BLIND BELIEF.

> "Man's credulous, and by his wavering mind
> All is received; it is a clay refined,
> With ease impressed; what strongest will appear
> Is dire surprise or unexpected fear."
>
> —*La Pucelle*, xl. 137.

BLINDED INTELLECT.
>"Your low, grovelling sect
>Debases man, unnerves his active soul,
>And makes it heavy, phlegmatic, and mean."
>>—*Mahomet,* xvi. 41.

BLIND MEN asking each other what light is; such is our quest after knowledge of the soul, xiii. 263.

BLISS IN BRAINLESSNESS. "For heaven's sake take care how you recover your senses; believe me, it would be the worst thing you ever did in your life."
>>—*The Prude,* xviii. 237.

BLOODY MARY, 1516-1558, xxvii. 111; a baby, born as the mother was burning at the stake, was cast back into the flames by order of the Catholic judge; hundreds of Protestants sent to the stake, xxvii. 113.

BLOOD SUCKERS; the legendary vampire survives in city stock brokers, who drain our substance in broad daylight, and live, not in cemeteries, but in fine palaces, xiv. 144.

BLUE BLOOD AND RED.
>"The blood of beggars and the blood of kings;
>Are they not equal in the sight of heaven?"
>>—*Olympia,* xv. 117.

BOABDIL, nephew of Abdallah, King of Granada, 1491, xxvi. 177; presented the keys of Granada to Ferdinand and Isabella, after a six years' struggle, 177.

BOCCACCIO, 1313-1375, xxvi. 51.

BODY, resurrection of the, a cannibalistic difficulty, xiii. 97.

BOILEAU ON LA FONTAINE, viii. 314, xxxvi. 66.

BOLDNESS.   "The strong and brave
>Are born to rule; the people to obey.
>Labor and courage conquer all."
>>—*Orphan of China,* xv. 217.

BOLINGBROKE, LORD, 1678-1751, how he effected the treaty between Queen Anne and Louis XIV., vii. 59; he doubted the existence of Moses, xii. 23; his doctrine that "all's for the best," 85.

BONDAGE.

> "Your laws are tyrants, and their barbarous rigor,
> Deaf to the voice of merit, to applause,
> To family and fame, throws down distinction,
> The senate grind you, and the people scorn."
>
> —*Brutus*, xv. 259.

BONIFACE VIII., Pope, 1228-1303, his lavish donations of Kingdoms and Bulls, xxix. 282.

BONFIRE, consign existing laws to a, and make new ones that will work quickly, effectually, and cheaply, xi. 79.

BOOKS, what we owe to the earliest writings, vi. 265; perils of writing and reading, 270.

BOOK-READING. "A person may be touched with the shining beauties of a work at the first reading, and afterwards condemn faults that had then escaped his notice." —*Jansenism*, xxi. 160.

BORGIA, CÆSAR, Archbishop, 1476-1507, son of Pope Alexander VI., his unsavory reputation, xxvi. 207; his villainies, 216.

BOSSUET, 1627-1704, the only eloquent man of his order, xiv. 225, xxi. 185; his style, xxx. 91, xxxvi. 65, xxxviii. 273.

BOSWORTH, battle of, 1415, death of Richard III., xxvi. 262.

BOUCHAGE, COUNT OF.

> "By turns a soldier and a saint was he,
> Now all for arms, and now a devotee,
> And bathed remorseless in his country's blood
> The hand he had devoted to his God."
>
> —*The Henriade*, xxxviii. 54.

BOUFLERS, MARSHAL, xxii. 259.

BOURDALOUE, PÈRE, his style, xxx. 90, xxxviii. 276.

BOURIGNON, ANTOINETTE, a wealthy fanatic, xxi. 162.

BOURLIE, ABBÉ DE LA, fanatical Huguenot, encouraged a revolt in the Cévennes after the expulsion; going to London in 1711, he was arrested for betraying the English ministry. At his examination he snatched a knife and wounded the Lord Treasurer Harley, and killed himself in prison, xxi. 133.

BRAHE, TYCHO, 1547-1601, astronomical discoveries, xxviii.
226.

"BRAHMIN AND A JESUIT." See DIALOGUES.

―― the Good. See ROMANCES.

―― and the Veda, xxix. 180-192.

―― origin of Purgatory, xii. 37.

BRAVERY OF CHARLES XII. while wounded, xx. 175.

BREAD TREE AND CORN, in the Philippines and America,
vi. 287.

BRIBERY.　　"The grand corrupter, gold,
　　　　Has bought him to our interest."
　　　　　　　　　　　　―Alzire, xvii. 46.

BRIDGET, ST., born in Sweden, settled in Rome, her letters
being dictated by an angel, xxv. 242.

BRINGING BACK THE DEAD to settle an estate, and letting
him return without offering so little as a glass of wine,
xiv. 149.

BRINVILLIERS, Marchioness, 1630-1676, who poisoned her
father, two brothers and sister, xxiii. 169.

BROTHERS-IN-LAW.　"The author would have us
believe that we are all brethren, all born equal and on
a level with each other; but 'tis an idle chimera; I
can't reconcile myself to his doctrine."
　　　　　　　　　　　　―Nanine, xviii. 104.

BROTHERHOOD.
"Sons of one God, in these our days of woe
Let's live like brothers while we dwell below."
　　　　　　　　　　―The Law of Nature, xxxvi. 34.

BRUCE, ROBERT, 1274-1329, King of Scotland, defeats the
English, xxv. 279.

BRUNO, ST., founder of the Carthusians, note, xli. 211.

BRUTE IMAGINATION, x. 167.

BUBBLES, FLOATING. "Women are strange creatures;
nay, and so are the men too."―The Prude, xviii. 195.

BUCCANEERS, demons who might have founded a power,
xii. 200.

BUCKINGHAM, GEORGE VILLIERS, 1592-1628, Duke of, his

influence over James I., his character and intrigues, xxviii. 255. See Richelieu.

BULL, Papal; the Bull *Unigenitus* and the Jesuits, vi. 307.

—— so called because Charles IV. of Luxemburg, King of Bohemia, who published the "Golden Bull" constitution in 1356, with a *bulla*, or golden seal, affixed to it, xxv. 237.

—— of Pope Julius II., permitting the eating of meat in Lent on payment of fees, xxvi. 182.

—— The White. See Romances.

BUMPTIOUSNESS not greatness, ix. 53.

BUNGO, the King of, his adoration of the Pope, xxix. 28.

BURGLARIOUS WAR.

> "To leave our bleeding country thus enslaved
> By European robbers, those assassins
> Who thirst for blood and gold, these proud usurpers,
> Who would extort by every cruel art
> Of punishment those riches which we hold
> More cheap, more worthless than themselves,
> 'Tis worse than death."　　*—Alzire*, xvii. 18.

BURIAL IN CONSECRATED GROUND, the church's exclusion of actors, xxxvii. 240.

BUSINESS LETTERS OF VOLTAIRE, xxxviii. 185.

BUSY-BODY, THE. "Let me advise you, madam, to make use of everything you know, and of everything you do not know."　　*The Scotch Woman*, xviii. 29.

BUSY WOMEN. "How very little women know of business."　　*—The Prodigal*, xix. 174.

BUTCHERS AND GLUTTONS, vegetarian philosophers can not prevail against them, xiv., 160.

BUTCHERY OF SWEDISH SENATORS, bishops and noblemen at the king's banquet, by order of the King and Archbishop, authorized by the Pope's bull, 1520, xxvii. 72.

BUTTERFLIES. "Live along with us without care or solicitude, never go too deeply into things, but float upon the surface."　　*—The Prude*, xviii. 250.

A PHILOSOPHICAL DICTIONARY.

VOL. VI.—Continued.

BABEL—CALENDS.

(End of Philosophical Dictionary.)

C

CALVINISM.
"Servetus, born in torments to expire,
By Calvin's self was sentenced to the fire."
—*The Law of Nature*, xxxvi., 32.

CALVINIST, TO THE SOUR.
" If, then, you needs must be damnation speed,
Be damned for pleasure, 'tis the wisest deed."
—*La Pucelle*, xl., 196.

"**Candide,**" or, the Optimist; I. 59-209.

CANILLAC, MARQUIS DE, xxiii. 202.

CANNIBALISM A MATTER OF TASTE, vii. 5; at the siege of Samaria, II. Book of Kings, vii. 11.

CANON LAW CONCERNING IMPOTENCE, x. 182; the gospels on divorce, 183; no Mosaic reference to it, 183; the cases of Henry IV. of Spain, Alfonzo of Portugal, and the Marquis de Langeais, 184.

CANON LAW, must be subject to civil law, xiii. 114.

CANTEMIR, PRINCE, of Moldavia, by treachery to the Turks, helps Charles XII. to rout the Czar, xx., 220.

CANTICLES OF SOLOMON, the only book of love from a Hebrew source, simple and beautiful but "rather strong as an allegory" of Christ and his Church, xiii. 247.

CANUTE OF DENMARK, d. 1036, called the Great, his greatest acts being cruelties, xxiv., 270.

CAPET, HUGH, d. 996, and feudal France, xxiv. 240; laws and customs, armor in battle, 243; eight centuries of Capet rule, 245.

CAPUCHIN MONKS, THE, and the Empress Catherine II., xii., 273.

CARDINAL, the stuff that makes a Cardinal, xiv. 93.

CARDINAL VIRTUES, fortitude, prudence, temperance, and justice; the last is the whole, if it includes beneficence, the others are but useful qualities, xiv. 161.

CARTERET LORD, 1690-1763, his warlike policy; an English army marches into Flanders, xxxiii. 82.

CASAUBON, ISAAC, on Peter's treatment of Ananias and Sapphira, xii. 159.

CASUIST, THE.

> "Never did fair appearance gild so well
> The specious covering of a happy falsehood.
> With what dexterity I played on him,
> And blended truth with artifice."
>
> —*Mariamne* xvi. 247.

CASUISTRY. "What after all is truth? a conformity with our own ideas; what one says is always conformable to the idea one has whilst one is talking, therefore, properly speaking, there is no such thing as a lie." "You seem to be an excellent logician."

> —*The Scotch Woman*, xviii. 29; note, xl. 190.

CATHERINE, wife of Peter the Great; her lowly origin and adventures, xx. 222.

CATHERINE II., EMPRESS, letter to Voltaire, on monkish intolerance, xii. 273.

CATHERINE OF SIENA, who received, in the fourteenth century, a ring and a diamond from Jesus to ratify their nuptials. Peter of Capua saw this saint "transformed one day into the figure of a man, with a little beard upon his chin, and this figure was exactly that of Jesus."   —*General History*, xxv. 242.

CAUTION. "She seems a most amiable girl, but in this world one should swear to nothing."

> —*Nanine*, xviii. 140.

CAVALIER, extraordinary leader of Huguenot fanatics, his character and methods pictured by Voltaire, who knew him, xxi. 135; a baker's boy able to negotiate a peace with Louis XIV. and accept a high salaried colonelcy, 137.

CELIBACY OF CLERGY, vii. 198.

CENSUS, by Moses, xii. 64; his people punished because David counted them, 65.

CENTAURS AND MONSTERS seen by Jerome and Augustine, xi. 175.

CERBERUS, the three-headed watch-dog of hell, x. 22.

CEREMONIES, curious observances, their causes and effects, vii. 207.

THE EMPERORS, WHOSE CAREERS ARE PIC-
TURED IN THE "ANNALS."

Charlemagne, first emperor, xxxi. 14; Louis le
Debonnaire, second emperor, 50; Lotharius, third, 62;
Louis II., fourth, 68; Charles the Bald, fifth, 74;
Louis III., the Stammerer, sixth, 77; Charles III., the
Fat, seventh, 78; Arnold, eighth, 88; Louis IV., ninth,
91; Conrad I., tenth, 91; Henry the Fowler, eleventh,
93; Otho the Great, twelfth, 96-111; Otho II., thirteenth, 111; Otho III., fourteenth, 116; Henry II,
fifteenth, 122; Conrad II., sixteenth, 131; Henry III.,
seventeenth, 135; Henry IV., eighteenth, 140; [see
Gregory VII., Pope] Henry goes to Canossa, 148;
Henry V., nineteenth, 160; Lotharius II., twentieth,
169; Conrad III., twenty-first, 172; Frederick I., Bar-
barossa, twenty-second; 177-206; Henry VI., twenty-
third, 207; Philip I., twenty-fourth, 215; Otho IV.,
twenty-fifth, 220; Frederick II., twenty-sixth, 227-
251; Conrad IV., twenty-seventh, 251; Rudolph I., of
Hapsburg, first Emperor of the house of Austria,
twenty-eighth Emperor, 267-281; Adolphus of Nas-
sau, twenty-ninth, 281; Albert I. of Austria, thir-
tieth, 285; Henry VII. of Luxemburg, thirty-first, 293.

Louis V. of Bavaria, thirty-second Emperor, xxxii.
5-33; Charles IV., thirty-third, 33-60; Wenceslaus,
thirty-fourth, 60; Frederick of Brunswick, thirty-fifth,
assassinated before his coronation, 69; Robert, Count
Palatine of the Rhine, thirty-sixth, 69; Joshua, thirty-
seventh, 77; Sigismund, King of Bohemia, Hungary,
and Brandenburg, 77-95; Albert II., of Austria, thirty-
eighth, 96; Frederick III. of Austria, thirty-ninth,
100-127; Maximilian, fortieth, 127-159; Charles V.,
forty-first, 159-245; Maximilian II., forty-third, 252;
Rudolph II., forty-fourth, 263-287; Matthias, forty-
fifth, 288; Ferdinand II., forty-sixth, 295, continued
in xxxiii. 259-274; Ferdinand III., forty-seventh,
xxxiii. 274; the Peace of Westphalia, 289; description

dred followers; advised by Poniatowski he enters on
intrigues, hoping to induce the Turks to join him
against the Czar, 191; cross purposes between host and
guest, 195; Charles ignores hints suggesting that he
should depart to his own country, 200; events in Poland; all the dominions of Charles now invaded by
Peter, 202; Louis XIV. friendly towards Russia, 203;
the treaty of The Hague, 1709, 204; triumphant entry
of Peter the Great into Moscow, 1710, with trophies
of his victories over Charles, 206; Sweden had lost
quarter of a million men in the wars, yet they won
a victory over the Danes at this time, 209; curious
system of choosing Viziers, their rise and fall by
seraglio intrigues, 211; Prince Cantemir of Moldavia
aids Charles by treachery towards their Turkish benefactor, and they inflict a defeat on the Czar near
the Pruth, 221.

Peter the Great falls in love with Catherine, an illit-
erate but remarkably able young woman, 223; her influence in securing good terms for the Czar, 227;
fury of Charles, who arrived too late to impose
his harsh intentions, 228; continued intrigues; the
Turks fail to coerce Charles into withdrawal, he makes
his house a fort, and when he is about to be ejected by
an army, he and his forty henchmen defend themselves and kill a number of their assailants before fire
destroys the house; Charles is at last captured and
made a prisoner, after having received incredibly
generous treatment, besides vast sums of money,
from the hospitable Turks, 264. Progress of intrigues,
quarrels and revolutions in the seraglio, 267; Poland
in further trouble, 269; Charles confined at Demirtash,
279; cruel destruction of the town of Altena by the
Swedes under General Stenbock, 284; pitiful fate of
the populace, their town burnt, and their women
and children forced to perish in the snow at midnight of January 9, 1713, 284; Charles at last leaves
the dominion of the Turks, escorted in royal style,

after enjoying five years sanctuary, with honors
worthy of a victorious rather than a broken monarch,
290; Charles arrives at Stralsund, November 21, 1714,
after sixteen days' travel without sleep on a bed, 295;
state of Europe since Charles had left Sweden; splendid career of Peter the Great and growth of his empire, 300.

VOL. XXI.

Misfortune follows Charles XII.; Wismar be-
seiged by German and Danish troops, while 36,000
Saxons and Danes march upon Stralsund, and the
Czar was threatening an invasion of Sweden, xxi., 5;
Charles' uphill fight on the isle of Rügen, 12; he is
wounded, and for the second time is saved by
Poniatowski, 14; besieged in Stralsund, Charles
works hard and is undismayed under fire, 16; he escapes at midnight, December 20, 1715, in a small
boat with ten followers, 18; he raised another army
and fleet, and instead of defending his own country,
he invaded Norway with 20,000 men, 21; jealousies
among the enemies of Charles, 23; his counsellor,
Goetz, advises him to purchase a peace from the Czar,
24; whose adviser and Prince Menzikoff persuade the
Czar, who agrees, 26; the Corsairs of Madagascar
offer their fleet to Charles, and Cardinal Alberoni, of
Spain, pledged his aid, 28; intrigues and alliances, 31;
Goetz and the Swedish Ambassador arrested in Holland and London, spoiling the grand scheme, 33. The
Czar makes friendly overtures to France during his
visit to Paris in 1717, 34; the Swedish envoys released,
whereupon Goetz successfully appeals to the Czar's
ambition, 37; his scheme for magnifying the currency,
39; incurs popular hatred but is trusted by the King,
40; Charles starts an expedition to Norway in Octo-
ber, 1718, 43; the winter siege of Frederikshall, 44;
Charles shows his mettle by neither eating nor drinking for five days, 44; while watching the making of
trenches Charles is instantly killed by a half-pound

grapeshot, which struck him on the right temple, 46;
Charles had experienced all the grandeur of prosperity
and all the hardships of adversity, without being soft-
ened by the one, or the least disturbed by the other,
47. His character, his evil influence on his country;
an extraordinary rather than a great man. Personal
characteristics, religion, 48. Goetz beheaded, by decree of the Senate of Stockholm, 52.

Letter of Voltaire to Marshal Schuelenburg, dated
1740, upon matters concerning Charles XII., 53.

Letter of Voltaire to M. Norberg,   Chaplain to
Charles XII., on his inaccurate Life of the King, 59.

CHARLES GUSTAVUS X., OF SWEDEN, xx. 18; xxxvii. 277.
See GUSTAVUS VASA, GUSTAVUS ADOLPHUS, PETER THE
GREAT.

CHARTER OF LIBERTY. "The true charter of liberty
is independence, maintained by force."—xiv. 155.

CHARTIER, ALAIN, 1390-1458; the first melodious poet of
France. Note, xl. 54.

CHARTREUX MONKS may not eat half an ounce of mutton,
but may devour the entire fortune of a family, xiii. 222.

CHASTITY, Vows OF, vii. 198.

CHASTISEMENT.   " Whate'er the gods
Have done but fills my soul with sad dismay."
                              —*Semiramis*, xvii. 219.

CHAULIEU, ABBÉ, xxxvi. 59, 279.

CHECKERED.
      "Oft man from good to hated evil flies,
      None in all moments virtuous are or wise."
                    —*The Law of Nature*, xxxvi. 30.

CHEEK, a medium for acquiring the gift of prophecy,
xiii. 19.

CHESTERFIELD, LORD, 1694-1773, on the manners of the gods,
v. 175.

CHEVALIER DE BARRE, tortured to death for singing impious
songs, in the eighteenth century, xiv. 119.

CHIGI, CARDINAL, sent to offer the Pope's apologies to
Louis XIV., xxii. 113; xxiii. 140.

COMMERCE.

"That minister, (Colbert) as wise as great
By luxury enriched the state,
He the great source of arts increased
From North to South, from West to East."
—*The Man of the World*, xxxvi. 173.

COMMUNION, HIGH.

"The mind let loose from its corporeal chains,
A conversation with its God maintains."
—*Thoughts on Newton*, xxxvi. 76.

COMPANIONSHIP.

"The only solid bliss that mortals know
Springs from the tender sympathy of hearts,
From the blest transports friendship's force imparts."
—*To Frederic the Great*, xxxvi. 253.

COMPANY IN SORROW.

"It pours some joy into the bitter cup
Of sorrow, thus to mix my tears with thine."
—*Orestes*, xvii. 71.

COMPENSATION.

"He has virtues that will recompense
His worst of faults."   —*Amelia*, xvi. 90.

COMPROMISE.

"Marriage is the greatest good, or the greatest evil;
There is no such thing as a medium in it."
—*The Prodigal*, xix. 161.

COMRADESHIP.

" What soldier, who e'er held his honor dear
Would wish for freedom whilst his chief remains
In slavery?"   —*Zaire*, xix. 37.

CONFISCATION, a Biblical precedent cited in a French court, vii. 233.

CONFUCIUS, B. C. 551-479, vii. 79; his pure morality; an able mathematician, xxiv. 20; his religion, 31; xxix. 171; xxxv. 270.

CONNOISSEURS have redeemed reputations which were misjudged by the vox populi, xiv. 58.

CONQUEROR CUPID.   "Henceforth
I have no laws, no friends, no king, but thine,
So love commands and love shall be obeyed."
                              —*Amelia*, xvi. 120.

CONQUESTS, FAIR.
"But most of love's bewitching draught beware,
The bravest hearts are conquered by the fair."
                              —*The Henriade*, xxxviii. 18.

CONQUEST OF ENGLAND by William of Normandy, xxiv. 269; he had no right to England nor even Normandy as an illegitimate, 271; a strong ruler and law giver; established schools, 274.

CONSCIENCE.
"Depend upon it there's a time the heart
To virtue's paths by instinct's force returns,
And when the memory of former guilt
With terror harrows up the frighted soul."
                              —*Olympia*, xv. 107.

CONSEQUENCES. "What has he to fear who does his duty."   —*Socrates*, xvi. 287.

CONSERVATIVES. "How hard a matter it is to discover truth in this world, and those who know it best are the last to divulge it."   —*Letters*, xxxviii. 178.

CONSOLATION. "The only comfort left me is—to doubt."   —*Alsire*, xvii. 29.

CONSTANTINE, EMPEROR, 274-337, a villain, but a man of sense and a just reasoner, vi. 21; how he attained power and established the Church, vii. 150; his times, character and career; master of the Church though unbaptized, and an unrepentant murderer, 246; he first tolerated, and then persecuted religionists, xiv.

CROSS, different sorts of nails shown as relics of the, xii. 46.

CROWNS OF THORNS.
> "Even in that hour of triumph and success,
> Even in the bosom of prosperity,
> The heart of majesty was pierced with grief."
> —*Semiramis*, xvii. 149.

CROWNS, The Man of Forty. See ROMANCES.

CRUSADES, THE, history of, xxv. 83; Palestine in the eleventh century, 88; captured by Omar, who built the great mosque in Jerusalem, 89; Peter the Hermit, 90; Pope Urban's ambition, 91; promises remission of sins and penalties to all who would ravage Palestine; two hundred and eighty thousand vagabonds and dissipated knights march "to defend Jesus Christ and exterminate the Jews," 93; the crusaders capture Jerusalem and massacre all but Christians, 102; Godfrey of Bouillon chosen Duke of Jerusalem, 104; wars of Turks and Christians, 106; crusaders cut to pieces by the troops of Solyman, 107; the Knights Templars, 107; failure of the first crusades, 108; incidental wars, 109; St. Bernard of Clairvaux, 110; disasters to the French, 113; Saladin, his noble character and victorious career, 114-121; the Christians plunder Constantinople and massacre the people, 123-146; capture of Damietta, 129; dread of Genghis Khan, 132; St. Louis a virtuous King, his early victories against England, 135; his rash and costly crusade, 137; is taken captive, returns in four years, 142; his wise rule, 143; he died while besieged by the Moors, aged fifty-five, with the piety of a monk and the courage of a hero, 144.

CRYING. "Ridiculous! I never wept in my life; our eyes were never given us for that purpose."
> —*The Scotch Woman*, xviii. 78.

CUISSAGE, the right of, on the marriage of common people, xiv. 66.

CUMOEAN, SYBIL, THE; introduced Christian doctrine, xiii. 207.

CUNEGUNDA, wife of Henry II. of Germany, walks barefoot over nine red hot ploughshares, unhurt, proving her fidelity, xxiv. 297.

CURFEW BELL, no tyrannical law; it was necessary to guard their rude wooden houses from fire, xxiv. 274.

CURIOSITY, highest prices paid to see brutal spectacles; the fearful torture-death of Damiens, viii. 44.

CURIOUS TABLE OF PRICES FOR CHURCH SANCTIONS, xiv. 68.

CURRENCY, xxxvii. 219.

CUSTOM. "The dominion of custom is much more extensive than that of nature, and influences all manners and all usages. It diffuses variety over the face of the universe."   —*General History*, xxx. 144; vii. 45.

CYPRIAN, ST., 200-258, his picture of the priests of his day, vii. 162.

CYRANO DE BERGERAC, xii. 126; xiii. 141, 170.

CYRUS, B. C. 590-529, the "Lord's Anointed" and an "illustrious robber," viii. 49.

CZAR PETER THE GREAT, 1672-1725, "is, perhaps, of all princes, the one whose deeds are most worthy of being transmitted to posterity."

                 —*Empire of Russia*, xxxiv. 5.

A PHILOSOPHICAL DICTIONARY.

VOL. VI.—Continued.

CAESAR—CALENDS.

CAESAR, B. C. 100-44, idolatrous worship of their tyrant by the French, 311.

CALENDS, early church feasts of Fools, Asses and Innocents. 314.

VOL. VII.

A PHILOSOPHICAL DICTIONARY.
CONTINUED.
CANNIBALISM—COUNCILS.

Americas, 153; efforts of the primitive society to found
a commune, 159; their love feasts degenerated, 161;
St. Cyprian pictures the worldliness of the priests of
his day, 162; six centuries of schisms, wars, and plunder, 163; Hildebrand as Pope, 164.

The Quakers return to primitive Christianity, 165;
William Penn and his colony, 166; his code more
liberal than those of Plato and Locke, 167; in his day
Philadelphia deserved its name, 168.

The split between the Latin and Greek churches,
170; bearded *versus* beardless priests, 173; the ortho-
doxy of blood puddings, 174; the Holy Sepulchre at
Easter, 177.

CHURCH OF ENGLAND, powerful because of its privileges,
178; freedom of its clergy, 179.

CHURCH property, growth of wealth in the early church,
180; where the once common fund goes, 182; monks
as slave-owners, 183.

CICERO, B. C. 106-43, an estimate of his life and career,
184.

CIRCUMCISION, Herodotus on, 191; adopted by the Jews
from the Egyptians, 193.

CLERK, Clergy, meaning of term "benefit of clergy," 197;
celibacy of, 198; Bishop Paphnucius held that marriage
is chastity, 199; second marriages by the clergy, 200;
Pope Gregory excommunicated married priests, 201;
Pius II. upheld the marriage of Popes, 201; Clerks of
the Closet became Secretaries of State, 202.

CLIMATE, its influence on mental activity, 203; physical
causes for modes of ceremonial worship, 207.

COHERENCE, Cohesion, Adhesion, Newton's theory of attraction, 210.

COMMERCE, the Portuguese once great in trade, 211; the
cause of England's power, 212.

COMMON SENSE, how blind faith and fear kill it, 214.

CONFESSION, a practice in Egypt, Greece, and among the
Jews, 216; scandals of public confession, 218; Louis
XI. and the Marchioness de Brinvilliers confessed be-

VOL. VIII.

A PHILOSOPHICAL DICTIONARY.
CONTINUED.
COUNTRY—CYRUS.

bloody spectacles, 44; the fearful torturing to death of Damiens, 47.

CUSTOMS, usages, law, justice; weights and measures vary according to locality, 48.

CYRUS, B. C. 590-529. Conflicting biographies of this "Lord's anointed," 49; propriety of cutting the head off the "illustrious robber," 53.

(End of Philosophical Dictionary.)

D

D'ALEMBERT, Dean le Rond, 1717-1783; his lucid style, xiii. 143.

DAMIENS, ROBERT FRANCIS, stabbed Louis XV. "for religion's sake," xxx. 233.

DAMNATION, eternal, threatened by Jesus but not generally believed in by the Jews, x. 25; of Kings, artists, and farmers by Mother Church, xxxvii. 249.

DAMNATION OF THE GOOD.

"Shall Aristides, Socrates the sage,
Solon, the guide and model of his age,
All be cast into the abyss of hell,
By the Just Being whom they served so well?
And shall you be in heaven, with glory crowned,
While crowds of cherubim your throne surround,
Because with monks a wallet once you bore,
In ignorance slept and greasy sackcloth wore?"
　　　　　　　　　　—*The Law of Nature*, xxxvi. 34.

DAMNED, THE.

"Love, talent, wit, grace, beauty, every age,
Great throng unnumbered, an immortal crew,
True heaven-born race, O Satan, made for you!"
　　　　　　　　　　—*La Pucelle*, xl. 176.

DANCE OF THE MASS, THE, quoted from St. John by the Second Council of Nice, xi. 232.

DANTE, 1265-1321, little read and less understood, because of his translators and interpreters, viii. 54; xxvi. 49.

D'ASSISSI, FRANCIS, ST., founder of the Franciscan Friars,

in 1210; world-wide spread of the order, xxxvii. 137;
xxxix. 260. See MONKS.

DATE OF THE NATIVITY DISPUTED, vii. 124.

DAUPHIN, from the province of Dauphiny, from one of its
kings having taken a dolphin for his arms, xxv. 299.

DAVID'S CONSCIENCE, after the murder of Uriah, in a state
of obduracy and darkness for a whole year, vii. 239;
portrayed as lover, poet, liar, vindictive conqueror,
murderer, adulterer, harpist, petty king, ancestor of
Mary and Jesus, and pardoned penitent, viii. 57.

—— his alleged wealth, amounting to some six thousand
million dollars; more money than was then circulating
through the whole world, xiii. 239.

DAZZLED. "The moment he became Mr. President, by
any troth, he was stuffed up with vanity and imperti-
nence."   —*The Prodigal*, xix. 146.

DEAD, BAPTISM OF THE, vi. 203.

DEAF HEAVEN.   "Cæsar's but a man,
Nor do I think that heaven would e'er disturb
The course of nature, or the elements
Rise in confusion, to prolong the life
Of one poor mortal."   —*Cæsar*, xix. 135.

DEATH'S MASKS.
                    "What is this phantom death,
That thus appals mankind? The wretch's hope,
The villain's terror, and the brave man's scorn."
                    —*Orphan of China*, xv. 189.

DEATH AS FRIEND.
"Without reluctance, and without regret,
The wise expect and meet him as a friend."
                    —*Orphan of China*, xv. 189.

DEATH, FEAR OF.
"Better to die than be afraid of death."
                    —*Cæsar*, xix. 136.

DEBATE.
"Much were their arguments with wisdom fraught;
Their words were gold, but they concluded naught."
                    —*La Pucelle*, xl. 44.

DEBORAH, Commander of the Jewish army, and the fate of the defeated Sisera, general over three hundred and ten thousand soldiers, vi. 213; note xl. 92; xli. 273.

DEBTS OF LOUIS XIV., xxxvii. 222.

DECADENCE.
"Soft Lucullus,
Sunk 'in the arms of luxury and sloth."
—*Catiline*, xvii. 247.

DECEIT.
"Can there on earth be hearts so base as e'er
To boast a passion which they never feel?"
—*Zaïre*, xix. 74.

DECEIVING THE PEOPLE, the Fakir Bambabef argues for it, and Whang, the Confucian, against it, ix. 123.

DEEDS, NOT CREEDS, a decision of the Court of Heaven, viii. 152.

DEEP DESCENT.   "Disgrace attends
On those alone who merit it—but know,
The blood of nobles, your patrician friends,
Debased by guilt, should rank below the meanest."
—*Catiline*, xvii. 281.

DEFEATS. "The loss of battles is not so much owing to the number of the killed, as to the timidity of those who survive."   —*Charles XII. of Sweden*, xx. 60.

DEFIANT NATURE. "Man is far too weak to conquer nature."   —*Orphan of China*, xv. 193.

DEITY; we believe by reason, not faith, viii. 326; it is the will of God that we should be virtuous, and not that we should be absurd, 328; controversies on Deity, xii. 205. See GOD.

DELIBERATION.
"Judgments too quickly made are oft unjust."
—*Catiline*, xvii. 273.

DELUGES, TRADITIONS OF, vii. 65; the Ark and Dove a Samothracian tradition, xiii. 163.

DELUSION.   "Fate ofttimes
Deceives the hearts of men, directs in secret
And guides their wandering steps through paths unknown;

Ofttimes it sinks us in the deep abyss
Of misery, and then raises us to joy."
—Orestes, xvii. 119.

DEMOCRACY, OR MONARCHY? "The government of
men is exceedingly difficult," viii. 75.

DEMONIACAL POSSESSION, killing the body to liberate the
spirit, viii. 84.

DEMOS.
"The multitude are ever weak and blind,
Made for our use, born but to serve the great,
But to admire, believe us, and obey."
—Mahomet, xvi. 28.

DENIS, ST., who walked with his decapitated head in his
hand, note, xl. 57; xli. 269.

DESCARTES, RENÉ, 1596-1650, and Newton; sketch of their
lives and systems of philosophy, xxxvii. 164; xxxviii.
281; note, xli. 56.

DESCENT OF JESUS INTO HELL, x. 33.

DESERT ISLANDS, problems for small societies on, xi. 91.

DESPAIR. "Against misfortune, injustice and poverty
there are arms that will defend a noble heart, but
there is an arrow that always must be fatal."
—The Scotch Woman, xviii. 26.

DESPOTISM.
"I hate our Eastern policy, that hides
Its tyrants from the public eye, to screen oppression."
—Zaire, xix. 32.

DESPOTISMS, PLAUSIBLE.
"I, too, my lord, am fond of liberty.
You languish for her, but enjoy her not.
Is there on earth, with all your boasted freedom,
Aught more despotic than a commonweal?"
—Brutus, xv. 258.

DESTINY. "I have necessarily the passion for writing
as I now do, and you have the passion for censuring
me; we are both equally fools, both equally the sport
of destiny," viii. 86.

DESTINY.

> "The orders of the gods must be obeyed;
> They never vary, are forever fixed,
> Unlike the changeful laws of humankind."
>
> —*Olympia*, xv. 116.

———

> "Spite of ourselves, our ways are noted down,
> Marked and determined."
>
> —*Sémiramis*, xvii. 218.

D'ESTRÉES, GABRIELLE, her influence over Henry IV., 1553-1610; xxviii. 95-100.

DETTINGEN, THE ENGLISH DEFEAT THE FRENCH AT, xxxiii. 150.

DEVIL EXPELLED BY THE SIGN OF THE CROSS, vii. 142; but the Jews had the same power, and now both Jews and Christians have lost it, 143.

—— gets into very agreeable society, x. 190.

———

> "The Devil, my dear, is full of spite."
>
> —*The Prude*, xviii. 196.

DEVOTEE, fancy picture of a, viii. 91.

———

> "She pours her daily incense at their altars,
> And wearies heaven with vows."
>
> —*Sémiramis*, xvii. 173.

DEVOTION. "She has a friendship for me, and that's better than money."

> —*Nanine*, xviii. 127.

"DIALOGUE BETWEEN MARCUS AURELIUS AND A RECOLLET FRIAR." See ROMANCES.

"—— between a Brahmin and a Jesuit." See ROMANCES.

"—— between Lucretius and Posidonius." See ROMANCES.

"—— between a Client and His Lawyer." See ROMANCES.

"—— between Madame de Maintenon and Mdlle. de L'Enclos." See ROMANCES.

"—— between a Savage and a Bachelor of Arts." See ROMANCES.

—— on Excommunication, xxxvii. 240.

DOOMED CITY, THE.
> "Was then more vice in fallen Lisbon found
> Than Paris, where voluptuous joys abound?"
> > —*The Lisbon Earthquake,* xxxvi. 9.

DOOMSDAY. the end of the world was to arrive before the disciples died, but it has not come yet. Was Jesus mistaken, or did He deceive? To suggest either would be blasphemy, viii. 232.

DON PEDRO THE CRUEL, 1334-1369, of Castile, his family troubles, xxvi. 5.

DOUBLE PROCESSION OF THE HOLY GHOST, vii. 303.

DOUBT.
> "As I grow older, I doubt of all things," xiv. 38.

DOWN-GRADE.
> > "Pomp and pride,
> Excess and luxury, the fruits of conquest,
> Are the time's vices." —*Catiline,* xvii. 237.

DRAKE, FRANCIS, 1545-1596, and Cavendish, sail round the world, xxviii. 18.

DRAMATIC CRITICISM.
> " I thought the comedy last night was an excellent one."
> " Detestable! Our taste grows worse and worse."
> > —*The Scotch Woman,* xviii. 11.

DRAMAS.

See Contents.

VOLS. XV—XIX.

MÉROPE.

VOL. XV.

PREFACES TO PLAYS.

DRAMATIC CONSTRUCTION, xxxix. 122-174. See PREFACES, xix. 235.

DREAD.
> "Fear is the natural punishment of guilt,
> And still attends it."   —*Sémiramis*, xvii. 212.

DREAMS, philosophy of, xiii. 256; of Anne, Princess of Cleves, which led to her conversion, xiv. 179.

DRESS, SECRET OF.
> "You seem extremely well dressed."
> "Plain, very plain."
> "But with taste."
>   —*The Prude*, xviii. 185.

DRUIDS, their human sacrifices, xxiv. 14.

DRYASDUSTS. "A set of rigid people who call themselves solid; gloomy geniuses, who pretend to judgment because they are void of imagination."
                    —*Essays*, xxxvii. 113.

DUBOIS, Cardinal and Prime Minister, 1651-1723; bad in sentiment, morals and conduct, xxi. 174; a jest to the people, a characterless worldling, xxx. 153.

DUELLING, a custom of the barbaric eighth century, xxiv. 142; xxx. 32; the first duel, note, xli. 99.

DU GUESCLIN, BERNARD, 1320-1380; a valiant knight, defeated Don Pedro and the English, as Constable of France; died 1380, and was buried with royal honors, xxvi. 13.

DUNKERS, THE, of Pennsylvania, vii. 169; a sect more

secluded from the world than Penn's Quakers, who reject the doctrine of original sin as impious, and that of hell as barbarous.

"The most just and inimitable of men." 170.

DUNKIRK, CAPTURE OF, by Condé, xxii. 43; siege of and surrender to the English, 87; purchased back from England by Colbert, xxii. 114.

DUMOULIN, DR., bequeathed these "two great physicians," simple diet and soft water, xiii. 39.

DUNS SCOTUS, 1265-1308, "The Subtle Doctor," xxvii. 139.

DUTCH REPUBLIC, the making of the, xxvii. 287; sea fights with England, xxii. 116.

DUTY. "I have done no more than was my duty."

—*Zaire*, xix. 35.

DYSPEPSIA. "This world is a hateful place!"

—*Nanine*, xviii. 107.

A PHILOSOPHICAL DICTIONARY.

VOL. VIII. DANTE—DRUIDS.

D.

DANTE, 1265-1321, little understood because of his commentators, little read because of his translators, viii. 54.

DAVID, Bayle's study of the divine favorite, 57; the magical virtue of olive oil as a regal hair dressing, 61.

DELUGE, Universal, pious reasons for belief in it, 70; its wonderful capacity, 71; learned reasonings on the tragical miracle, 73.

DEMOCRACY, pros and cons of, 75; the Athenian republic banished Cimon, Aristides, Themistocles, and Alcibiades, and killed Phocion and Socrates; the monarchy of Macedon was responsible for two hundred years of atrocious crimes, 76; the republic, when too late, made apologies and reparation, 79; the noble example of Switzerland, 81; kingdom of the Jews, 83.

DEMONIACS, the "sacred disease" 83; curing the patient

(End of Philosophical Dictionary.)

E

EARTHQUAKES.

"When the earth gapes my body to entomb
I justly may complain of such a doom.
* * * * * *
Say, what advantage can result to all
From wretched Lisbon's lamentable fall?"
                —*The Lisbon Earthquake*, xxxvi. 10.

ELECTRICITY, is it not (asks Voltaire) the source of all
sensation, and is not sensation the origin of thought?
ix. 93.

ELEUSINIAN MYSTERIES, THE, x. 205.

ELIZABETH, Queen of England, 1533-1602, tolerant of all
beliefs, xxvii. 115; xxviii. 20; her many personal and
political troubles, 22; imprisoned by her sister, Mary,
23; when proclaimed Queen she refuses the hand of
Philip of Spain; became supreme head of the church,
24; compelled Mary Stuart to drop the title, Queen
of England, 27; Philip stirs up troubles in Ireland,
which she suppressed; her judicial murder of Mary
Stuart; a reign of justice, wisdom and progression,
30. See MARY, QUEEN OF SCOTS.

ELOQUENCE, its nature and history, viii. 197; in verse is of
all arts the most difficult and uncommon, xv. 7.

EMBLEMS, good and bad; examples from the pagans and
Hebrews, viii. 222.

EMPERORS QUAN-CUM, KIN-CUM, AND KIN-CUM QUANCUM,
of China, xxix. 144; the Tartar hordes, 148; List-
ching, the last of the emperors, 151.

"Empire, Annals of the." See "ANNALS."

EMPTY PRETENDERS. "I would prefer a fool to cox-
comb at any time."   —The Prodigal, xix. 145.

"ENCYCLOPEDIA," THE, a remarkable circumstance relating
to literature.   —Essays, xxxvii. 85.

ENCYCLOPEDISTS, the lovers of truth, xii. 182, 191.

ENGLAND, CHURCH OF, vii. 178; xxxix. 212.

—— grew rich after liberating the "poor" monks of their
accumulated wealth, xiii. 8; in the ninth century, xxiv.
174; feudalism in, xxv. 45; during the Reformation,
xxvii. 107.

—— and Ireland given by King John to the Pope in 1213,
viii. 164.

after the death of Elizabeth; James VI. of Scotland
and I. of England, asserter of the "divine right" which
led to the misfortunes of his family and the nation,

At Paris I had been a Christian; here
I am a happy Mussulman; we know
But what we learn."   —*Zaïre*, xix. 27.

ENVIABLE. "A young and beautiful girl, who at the
same time is good natured and sincere, is sure to dis-
please her whole sex."   —*Nanine*, xviii. 109.

ENVY.

"Of pride and folly envy is the child,
Stubborn, perverse, intractable, and wild."
          —*Envy*, xxxvi. 183.

—— "Better excite envy than pity," viii. 246.

EPICTETUS, first century, a pure theist, x. 137.

EPIPHANIUS THE SAINT, 310-403, his slanders against his
friends, xi. 56.

EPISCOPATE, THE, how it originated, xxiv. 129.

EPISCOPUS.

"A pampered prelate, one with fat o'ergrown,
Triple-chinned, much to apoplexy prone."
          —*The Temple of Friendship*, xxxvi. 72.

EPISTLES OF PAUL, curiosities of the, xii. 148.

EQUALITY, its unfortunate limitations, viii. 265.

—— of conditions, i. 283.

—— "As men, we are all equal; as members of society we
are not. This equality does not destroy subordination."
          —*Essays*, xxxvii. 231.

EQUALLY FATED.   "Rich and poor,
The monarch and the slave, are equal all
By nature; all alike to sorrow born,
Each has his share, and in the general wreck
All duty bids us is to save our own."
          —*Orphan of China*, xv. 197.

ERASMUS, 1467-1536, on Aaron and Peter the Apostle, xxx.
69.

EROTIC PHILOSOPHY, on the elements of love, xi. 141.

"Essays on Literature, Philosophy, Art, History," xxxvii.

VOLTAIRE'S ACADEMY SPEECH..................... 5
VOLTAIRE'S FUNERAL EULOGIUM.................. 27
THE ANTI-LUCRETIUS OF CARDINAL DE POLIGNAC... 48

ESTEEM. "There are those whom one may esteem and yet laugh at, and make fools of, is it not so?"
—*The Prude*, xviii. 198.

Estrées, Gabrielle d', note xli. 105.

Eternal Punishment for the sins of a few short years, a Christian, not a pagan doctrine, x. 30. See Hell, Dunkers.

Eugene, Prince of Savoy, 1663-1736, xxii. 250; a great general ill-treated by France, who shook the power of Louis XIV. and the Turks, xxiii. 5; at Ramillies, 54; defeated at Denain, 99; note, xl. 118.

Eunuchs, only one famous general, and two eminent scholars, xxx. 274.

Europe in the thirteenth century, xxv.; England, Scot-

With acclamations loud, and songs of joy.
They little know the grief that wrings thy heart."

—*Mérope*, xv. 84.

EXTORTION by monks, through the ghost of a woman wrongly buried in consecrated ground, xiv. 167.

A PHILOSOPHICAL DICTIONARY.

VOL. VIII., Continued. EASE—EZEKIEL.

E.

EASE, the art and artifice of, viii. 174.

ECLIPSE at the Crucifixion, 176. See DIONYSIUS.

ECONOMY, rural; the thrifty Abraham and his descendants, 181.

—— of speech, in Paul, 184; in Jerome, 186; in Augustine, 187; in Irenæus, 188; in Tertullian, 189.

ELEGANCE in poetry and oratory, 190.

ELIAS or Elijah, and Enoch. Various accounts and interpretations of their departure without death, 193.

ELOQUENCE. Nature makes men eloquent, 197; Aristotle on the art, 199; Cicero, Demosthenes, Quintilian, Bossuet, Bourdaloue, Massillon's bold figure, 203; a hint to preachers, 204.

EMBLEMS, figures, allegories, symbols. Universally employed by the ancients, 207; the most beautiful of all emblems describing God, by Timæus, quoted by Plato, 209; examples from Ecclesiastes, Song of Solomon, Jeremiah, Ezekiel, Hosea, 209.

ENCHANTMENT, magic conjuration, sorcery. Serpent charming, 222; awaking the dead, 226; sorceries and love philtres, 230.

END OF THE WORLD. Beliefs of the pagans, 232; of the Apostles and the Egyptians, 235.

ENTHUSIASM, by Ignatius and Francis Xavier, 238; Alexander's Feast, by Dryden, the noblest ode of enthusiasm, 243.

ENVY, emulation kept within the bounds of decency, 245.

EPIC poetry; Hesiod's *Works and Days*, equal in merit

(End of Philosophical Dictionary.)

F

FADING GLORY.
> "Rome soon must fall;
> But ere I will attempt to be her master
> I will extend her empire and her glory
> And if I forge my country's chains, at least
> Will cover them with laurels."
> *—Catiline,* xvii. 249.

FAIR-WEATHER FRIENDS. "My numerous foes I heed not, 'tis my friends I have most cause to dread."
> *—Catiline,* xvii. 242.

FAIRFAX, SIR THOMAS, 1612-1671, general of the Parliamentarian forces, xxviii. 285.

FAITH, how the Hindoo acquires, viii. 327.

—— "I see the hand of God in all our woes,
> And humbly bend myself before that power
> Who wounds to heal and strikes but to forgive."
> *—Alsire,* xvii. 62.

FAITH CURES.
> "Baits to allure the unthinking multitude,
> By knaves invented and by fools believed."
> *—Semiramis,* xvii. 177.

—— POWER OF.
> "No man but fought divested of all fear,
> Their bosoms glowed with superstitious pride,
> For each believed the Lord was on his side."
> *—xl.* 136.

FAITHFUL FRIEND. "Where'er the gods lead, friendship shall triumph o'er the woes of mortals and the wrath of heaven."   *—Orestes,* xvii. 145.

FALLEN FROM GRACE.
> "O, were I gifted with an iron tongue,
> In ceaseless motion, still would ne'er be sung,
> Dear friend, the number of those saints who roam
> In realms of hell, their everlasting home."
> *—The Maid of Orleans,* xl. 180.

FALLEN IDOLS.
> "Fear not the people, though they are doubtful now,
> Whene'er the idol falls, they will detest him."
> *—Cæsar,* xix. 118.

FALLIBILITY.
"The deepest wisdom
Is oft deceived." —*Cæsar*, xix. 98.
"FALSE DECRETALS, THE," viii. 68.
—— Messiahs, a clerical review of their claims, xi. 249.
—— sight common, but it takes a distorted intellect to mistake a coffee pot for a church, xiv. 252.

FAME.
"Such is oft the fate
Of the best sovereigns; whilst they live respect
Waits on their laws, their justice is admired,
And they like gods are served, like gods adored,
But after death they sink into oblivion."
—*Œdipus*, xvi. 156.

FAMILY RIGHTS AND WRONGS in the eighth and ninth centuries, xxiv. 145.

FAMINE, Horrors of. —*The Henriade*, xxxviii. 153.

FANATICISM, a malady of the mind, caught in the same way as small-pox, but a more destructive scourge, ix. 16; xxxviii. 249, 262. See BARTHOLOMEW MASSACRE, TOLERATION.

FASHION mostly dictated by fancy rather than taste, xiv. 47.
"Fashion, Madam, is despised by wisdom; I will obey its ridiculous commands in my dress, perhaps, but not in my sentiments; no, it becomes a man to act like a man, to preserve to himself his own taste and his own thoughts." —*Nanine*, xviii. 97.

FASHIONABLE RELIGION.
"With such as you, salvation's for the great,
The poor alone can miss a blissful state."
—*The Nature of Virtue*, xxxvi. 190.

FATALISM. "Ye immortal powers
That guide our steps, it is to your decrees
That I submit." —*Sémiramis*, xvii. 208.

FATE. "'Tis not in mortals to resist their fate."
—*Orphan of China*, xv. 217.

—— of philosophy to be persecuted, xii. 188. See DESTINY, LIBERTY, FREE WILL.

FATES, THE, their infernal occupation, x. 22.

xxxiii. 225; the English salute their French enemy
and invite them to fire first; the French reply, "Gentle-
men, we never fire first, do you begin," 238; after all
but losing the battle the French, under Marshal Saxe,
snatched final victory, the King and his sons witness-
ing the fight, 257. This victory determined the fate
of the war and paved the way for the conquest of the
Netherlands, xxxvi. 156. See "WAR OF 1741."

FONTEVRAND, ABBEY OF, note, xl. 131.

FOOLS.

"Fools are incapable of love."
—*The Prude*, xviii. 172.

—— "The more fools there are, the more one laughs."
—*The Prude*, xviii. 177.

FOOL FRIENDS.

" To keep my friends within the pale of prudence
Will cost me much more trouble."
—*Catiline*, xvii. 244.

FORCE, physical and mental, fire which waxes colder with
age, ix. 100.

—— decides popular doctrine, until reason is strong enough
to disarm force, xiv. 32.

—— and liberty; churches seek to coerce, but religion pre-
sumes free choice, xiii. 115.

FOREIGN NAMES GIVEN BY THE JEWS TO THEIR DEITY, xiv.
113.

FORGETTING, ART OF.

"My philosophy is, remember nothing."
—*The Prude*, xviii. 234.

FORMALITY AND CEREMONIES flourish in proportion to the
barbarism of people, vii. 39.

FORTUNE. "Fortune makes us blindly play her terrible
game, and we never see beneath the cards," xiv. 92.

FORWARD.

"Thou art entered in the paths of glory,
And to retreat were fatal."   —*Catiline*, xvii. 257.

FOUQUET, NICOLAS, Marquis of Belle Isle, 1615-1680, finan-
cier under Louis XIV. He squandered the revenues

A PHILOSOPHICAL DICTIONARY.—Continued.

VOL. VIII. FABLE—FALSITY.

F.

VOL. IX. FANATICISM—FRIVOLITY.

Confucian, who said that deception is wrong, 123; the politic necessity for a God, 128.

FREE-WILL, we do an act, or we do not, not being free to will that we won't do either, 128; liberty is the power of acting; how will is formed, who knows? 130.

FRENCH LANGUAGE; its origin and growth, 132.

FRIENDSHIP, the marriage of the soul, liable to divorce, 137.

FRIVOLITY, without it existence would be too depressing to be endured, 139.

(End of Philosophical Dictionary.)

G

GABRIELLE D'ESTRÉES, 1571-1599, and Henry IV., "THE HENRIADE," xxxviii. 132.

GALILEO, 1564-1642, Kepler, Newton, Copernicus, xiv. 40.

—— " Poor Galileo, harassed in old age,
Who claims forgiveness with a heart contrite,
Justly condemned for being in the right."
—La Pucelle, xl. 108, 127.

GALLANTRY, how it degraded the French drama, xxxvii. 130.

GARDEN OF EDEN, why we were chased out by the best of all possible Gods, xii. 82.

GASSENDI, PIERRE, 1592-1655, xxxviii. 287.

GENERAL HISTORIES, Concluding Notes on the, xxx. 247. See "ANCIENT AND MODERN HISTORY."

GENIUS IS CAPACITY, ix. 196; is possessed by few men and fewer women, xii. 226.

—— the English, xxxvi. 100.

GENTLENESS.   "Gentle means
Are ever the most powerful."
—Alzire, xvii. 43.

GENTLE BREED.

" Be courteous and affable to the poor; are they
Not men as well as yourself?"
—Nanine, xviii. 148.

GENTLE ILLUSION.
> " Since to error we're consigned
> Let us some pleasing errors find."
>   —*To* .... xxxvi. 211.

GENGHIS KHAN, 1162-1227 rise of, xxv. 132; head of the
Tartar hordes, 1220, 153; his religious and military
discipline, 155; a great statesman and conqueror, de-
stroys Bokhara, 158; had subdued half of China and
Hindostan, Persia and Russia in eighteen years, 159;
Died at seventy, 161; xxix. 262.

GEOMETRY, the claims of Descartes and Newton examined, xxxvii. 169.

GERMAN EMPIRE, THE, and its fiefs, xxiv. 216. See OTHO
THE GREAT.

GERMANY UNDER RUDOLPH II., 1576, a student of astronomy under Tycho Brahe, xxviii. 226; its thirty years'
war, 235.

GERMINATION. "Not that I'm in love with her, but
there is no parting from her without some uneasiness,
a kind of anxiety I never felt before; there's something
very extraordinary in it."
>   —*The Scotch Woman*, xviii. 85.

GEWGAWS.
> " Gewgaws which strike the vulgar eyes,
> But which all men of taste despise."
>   —*The Temple of Taste*, xxxvi. 47.

GHOSTS. "Prodigies (omens) never appear to those
who dread them not."   —*Sémiramis*, xvii. 177.

—— of the Saints scatter death among those who meddled
with their tombs, xiii. 59.

GIANT, story of the terrible, never seen, therefore fervidly
believed in, ix. 30.

GIDEON, his masterly strategical tactics, note, xl. 93.

GIFTS OF SOVEREIGNTIES TO THE POPES, Italy, Rome, Naples,
England and Ireland, viii. 156.

GIRARD, JEAN BAPTISTE, a Jesuit who was guiltless of
sorcery, note, xl. 91.

Fatal to happiness is either scheme,
Bliss never was found in the extreme."
                    —*The Nature of Pleasure*, xxxvi. 245.

GOLD-PLATED FAULTS. "Well, no matter; what does
it signify? All these faults are nothing when people
are rich."   —*The Prodigal*, xix. 146.

GOLDEN SILENCE. "At court, my dear, the most necessary art is not to talk well, but to know how to
hold one's tongue."   —*The Tatler*, xviii. 264.

GOLDSMITH, OLIVER, 1728-1774, his deftly expressed epi-
gram, xiv. 234.

—— on Voltaire, i. 32.

GOOD COMPANY. "This world is composed of knaves,
fanatics, and idiots, among whom there is a little
separate society called Good Company."
                    —*Essays*, xxxvii. 251.

—— "Plundered! by whom? how? when? where? Oh
from mere goodness of heart; our thieves were mighty
honest creatures, amiable triflers, gamesters, bottle
companions, agreeable story-tellers, men of wit and
women of beauty."   —*The Prodigal*, xix. 185.

GOOD-DOING.
            " My heart once more
Shall taste its noble happiness, the best
And fairest treasure of the virtuous mind,
The happiness to succor the oppressed."
                    —*Mariamne*, xvi. 218.

GOOD FELLOWS, the free-thinker Bishop Lavardin founded
the order of, xii. 116.

GOOD SENSE OF THEISM, which never persecutes, xiv. 80.

GOERTZ, HENRY DE, the able counsellor of Charles XII. of
Sweden, xxi. 21; advises the King to purchase a peace
from the Czar, 24; his grand scheme to gain allies
for the King, 29; arrested by the States General of
France, 33; released, and forms a plan to gain a peace
in the interest of the Czar, 37; raises money by putting
the value of one copper cent up to that of eighty, 38;

is hated by the people but trusted by the King, 40;
after the death of Charles, is beheaded, by decree, of
the Senate at Stockholm, 52.

GOSLIN, BISHOP, a ninth century man of valor with battle
axe and arrows, xxiv. 171.

GOSPEL OF THE INFANCY, and fifty other conflicting gospels in the early history of Christianity, vii. 112; the
Early Fathers and the false gospels, ix. 268; the gospel according to Nicodemus, x. 34; St. John's Gospel,
its philosophy borrowed from Plato, x. 55.

GOSSIP. "Ay, but the world will talk, madam."
                              —*The Prude*, xviii. 205.

GOURDS, why they grow high here and low there, ix. 303.

GOVERNING BADLY under good laws, ix. 277.

GOVERNMENT SYSTEMS AND THEORIES, the ideal yet to be
found, xiii. 332.

—— of Louis XIV. xxiii. 230.

—— thoughts on, xxxvii. 226.

GRAFTING CHRISTIAN MEANINGS into pagan superstitions,
xiii. 58.

GRAND MONARQUE, THE, his personal appearance and manner, xxiii. 114.

GRASPERS.
    "The greedy Crassus, grasping his large heaps
    Of ill-got wealth, enough to purchase Rome
    And all her venal sons."   —*Catiline*, xvii. 247.

GREAT FRIENDS.
    "I know the great too well. In their misfortunes
    No friends so warm, but in prosperity
    Ungrateful oft, they change to bitterest foes;
    We are the servile tools of their ambition,
    When useless, thrown aside with proud disdain."
                              —*Brutus*, xv. 251.

GREAT MEN. "Characters of great men are always
viewed in a false light during their lifetime."
                              —*Essays*, xxxvii. 147.

GREATNESS, a hack-word commonly misapplied to medioc-
rity, ix. 319.

—— " 'Tis but a step from triumph to disgrace."
                              —*Cæsar*, xix. 98.

GREATNESS OF A NATION.
  " That reverence and attachment to the State,
    That sacred name of country, which awakes
    The sense of honor in each patriot breast."
                              —*Catiline*, xvii. 266.

GREECE, under the Ottomans, xxx. 11.

GREEK CHURCH, state of the, before Charlemagne, xxiv.
    89; ceremonial differences between it and the Latin
    Church; their quarrels were over words more than
    principles, 90; image worship led to imaginary miracle
    working, 92.

—— the, of Russia, its area and strength, xxxiv. 62.

—— drama, xxxvi. 131.

—— Empire, fall of the, Michael Palæologus, his unworthy
    statesmanship in submitting the claims of the Greek
    Church to the Popes, xxvi. 87; Sultan Amurath, 89.

—— Latin and German words signifying soul, xiii. 266.

GREEKS, of all the people in the world, had the quickest
    feeling, xv. 6.

GREGORIAN CALENDAR, THE, its correction of the Julian,
    xxix. 24.

GREGORY VII., POPE, d. 1085, the firebrand of Europe, ix.
    329; rise of Hildebrand, the famous Pope, xxv. 7;
    absolves King Robert after his excommunication,
    xxiv. 262; ix. 329. See HILDEBRAND; HENRY IV., EM-
    PEROR.

—— IX., Pope, "THE HENRIADE," xxxviii. 61.

GRIEF.
        " We seldom try to mitigate a grief
          Which we contemn."   —*Amelia*, xvi. 139.

GRIEF'S SILENT LANGUAGE, tears, xiv. 69.

GRISEL, ABBÉ, and Abbé la Coste, note, xli. 195.

GRIT.   " Wrongs unrevenged
        To them are insupportable, and death
        More welcome far than infamy."
                              —*Orphan of China*, xv. 233.

GROPERS IN THE DARK.
> "These priests are not what the vile rabble think them,
> Their knowledge springs from our credulity."
>   —*Œdipus*, xvi. 187.

GROTIUS, HUGO, 1583-1645, on the rights of man, xiii. 108;
    xxix. 63.

GRUB STREET. The low state of hack writing in the eight-
    eenth century; libelling as a livelihood, xxx. 152.

GUESSES at the origin of the universe, xii. 83. See GOD,
    EVIL, FREE WILL, LIBERTY.

GUISE, DUKE OF, the conspiracy of 1560, xxviii. 42, 72, 74;
    assassinated, 83; "*The Henriade*," xxxviii. 40.

GUSTAVUS ADOLPHUS, 1594-1632, a conqueror, xx. 16; per-
    formed the deeds for which Cardinal Richelieu got
    the credit, 17; xxix. 73.

GUSTAVUS, VASA, 1496-1560, a great soul, a born monarch,
    xx. 15; delivered his people and was made King;
    substituted Lutheranism for Catholicism, 16.

GUYON, MADAME, 1648-1717, and Quietism; the good
    woman who brought a torch to burn Paradise and
    a bowl of water to extinguish hell fire, that God
    should no longer be worshipped through hope or
    fear, xiv. 205. See FENÉLON, QUIETISM.

GYPSIES, Egyptians, Bohemians, xxx. 50.

A PHILOSOPHICAL DICTIONARY.

VOL. IX.—Continued—GALLANT—GREGORY.

G.

GALLANT, various shades of meaning, 140.

GARGANTUA, THE GREAT; the Seine still exists from which
    he drank, yet there are doubting Thomases who re-
    fuse credence to his historian, Rabelais, 142.

GAZETTES, pioneers of modern newspapers, 146.

GENEALOGY, the unsatisfactory work of Matthew and Luke,
    149; Buddha born of a virgin, 153; impregnation
    through the ear, say Augustine and Pope Felix, 155;
    Adam the ancestor of Mahomet, 158.

H

—— criticism of its plan, xxxix. 122-174.

HANGMAN, THE, a doubtful benefactor, viii. 282.

HAPPENINGS. "By what arm
God sends us help, it matters not; for justice
With wisdom oft conspires to draw advantage
Alike from our misfortunes, and our crimes."
—*Zaïre*, xix. 39.

HAPPIER THAN WOMEN? Are men, x, 6.

HAPPINESS.
"I am distracted with a thousand cares.
. . . . When I was a poor unknown
I was more happy." —*Orphan of China*, xv. 215.

—— Make the most of it while it lasts, ix. 252.

HAPPY AGES, FOUR, those in which the arts were carried
to perfection, xxii. 5.

HAPPY SOULS. "Those who want nothing never can
be poor." —*The Scotch Woman*, xviii. 35.

HAROUN-AL-RASCHID, contemporary with Charlemagne,
xxiv. 62.

HARPIES, THE, note, xli. 259.

HASTEN SLOWLY. "I judge not with the hasty multitude." —*Œdipus*, xvi. 176.

HASTINGS, BATTLE OF, 1066, xxiv. 272.

HEALTH, TO RESTORE, simple diet and soft water, xiii. 39.

—— "Goddess who dost make blest the earth,
Health, who to temperance owest thy birth."
—*To President Hénault*, xxxvi. 284.

HEALTHY OR WISE. "A gracious God should make
his creatures happy." —*Pandora*, xvii. 302.

HEART, THE.
"Thus God, to whom each man his being owes,
In every heart the seeds of virtue sows."
—*The Law of Nature*, xxxvi. 26.

HEART-BREAK. "The heart oppressed is ever diffi-
dent." —*Alzire*, xvii. 22.

HEART-WHOLE.
"I'd sooner die; my life's at thy command
But not my heart." —*Amelia*, xvi. 121.

HEAVEN, curious conceptions of the ancients, x. 9.

HEAVEN'S SANCTION.

"That old pretense through all revolving time,
Divine religion, veiled the horrid crime."
—*The Henriade*, xxxviii. 42.

HEAVEN-SENT? "O, heaven! what woes dost thou inflict upon me."   —*Zaïre*, xix. 72.

HEBREW, the Fathers of the Church ignorant of Hebrew, except Jerome, Origen, and Ephrem, xiii. 19.

HEBREWS, the remarkable nation, x. 266; their history, xxi. 193; philosophy, 207; idolatry, 208. See JEWS.

HELL, as constructed by the Greeks, x. 21; and reconstituted by Jesus, 24-33.

HEN-ROOST a perfect representation of a monarchy, xi. 87.

"**Henriade, The,**" Epic of France, in Ten Cantos; Dedications to Louis XIV. and Queen Caroline of England, xxxviii. Introduction, 5.

Canto i. p. 9; ii. 23; iii. 38; iv. 53; v. 70; vi. 83; vii. 96; viii. 115; ix. 132; x. 144.

HENRY IV. OF FRANCE, 1553-1610, hero of "The Henriade;" before he was King, defiance of the Pope, xxviii. 79; his victory at Coutras, 80; born to trouble, 91; in a battle at fourteen, 1569; three years a prisoner of state, often in extreme destitution, succeeded to the throne on the murder of Henry III., 92; a rival King set up against him, gives battle to armies with a devoted handful of men, 93; defeated the Leaguers at Ivry by personal bravery, 94; the white plume of Navarre a merciful victor, 95; besieges Paris, 95; his amour with Gabrielle D'Estrees, 96, 100; intrigues of Philip II., 97; Henry drives the Duke of Parma out of France, 97; for reasons of state Henry becomes a Catholic, 99; "his conversion doubtless secured his eternal welfare, but it added nothing to his right to the crown," 101; entered Paris as King, 1594, 102; yet had the enmity of Pope and church, had to fight for his existence against armies and would-be assassins, 103; success at last, 104; "the bravest, most merciful, most upright, most honest man of his age," 105; convenes an assembly of the states-general, 106; is given a fine army, with which he drives out Spanish invaders of Amiens, 108; his beneficent reign, what he did for the nation, 109; motives of those who sought his murder, 115; is assassinated by Ravaillac, a fanatical mendicant friar, 1610, 121. See MEDICI, MARY DE.

—— and the Pope, their injustice to Ferrara, ix. 45; anecdotes of Henry, v. 177; a soldier lover, xxx. 273, 276, Ravaillac, 281; note, xli. 104.

HENRY THE FOWLER, 929; a worthy prince, xxiv. 219.

HENRY III. OF FRANCE, 1551-1589, and the murder of the Duke of Guise, xxviii. 76; is assassinated by a friar, 88.

HENRY II. OF ENGLAND, 1133-1189, xxix. 252.

HENRY V. OF ENGLAND, 1388-1422, battle of Agincourt, xxvi. 24; King of France and England, died in his thirty-fourth year, 31.

HENRY VII. OF ENGLAND, 1456-1509, his avarice, shrewdness, and success, xxvi. 264.

HENRY VIII. OF ENGLAND, 1491-1547, and the ecclesiastical upset, xxvii. 92; his experiments in marriage and divorce, 93; his theological battles with the

HERODOTUS, B. C. 480-408, his amazing stories on circumcision, vii. 191; viii. 120; his "history," x. 72; his firsthand testimony is trustworthy but not what he relates on the authority of the Egyptians, xxi. 278; xxxvii. 257.

HIDDEN SPRINGS.

"Our actions oft, even in our great concerns
Are but effects which from our passions spring;
Their power tyrannic we in vain disguise,
The weak is oft a politician deemed."

—*Olympia*, xv. 113.

HIGH AND LOW. "We have all our weaknesses."

—*Catiline*, xvii. 266.

HIGHLANDERS, SCOTCH, the only people on earth who dress in the military garb of the ancient Romans, xxiv. 123.

HILDEBRAND, POPE GREGORY VII. d. 1085, his rise and career, xxv. 7; his threat of excommunication against all laymen who conferred benefices and clerics who accepted them, 9; denounces the King of France and summons Emperor Henry IV. to Rome to answer charges, 10; who caused the Pope to be imprisoned and deposed, 12; Gregory in reply deposed the emperor, who was seized by rebel princes, and held for trial before the Pope, 14; Henry, in penitence, crosses the Alps with a few servants and offers his submission to the Pope at Canossa, whose guards stripped the emperor and robed him in haircloth, in which condition, and barefoot, he had to wait, in January, 1077, and fast three days before he was allowed to kiss the Pope's feet, 14; Gregory granted him absolution but held him for trial, which created sympathy for Henry, who headed a Lombardy army against the Pope, while the Pope was raising all Germany against Henry, and ex-communicated him again, 1078, presenting the crown to Rudolph, 16; Henry replied in 1080 by convening a council of Bishops, who excommunicated and deposed Pope Gregory, electing Guibert in his stead, and as deposed emperor, he headed an army against Rudolph, 17; who was defeated by Godfrey of Bouillon, 18; in 1083 Henry laid siege to Rome and ultimately took it, the Pope fortifying himself in the Castle of St. Angelo, where he defied and excommunicated Henry for the third time; the city was ravaged by the soldiers; Gregory died in 1085, his memory detested by Kings, but the Church made him a saint, 22; Henry was deposed in 1106 and died in poverty, his body being cast out of its church grave by the son who had betrayed him to his enemies, 24. See vii. 164; GREGORY VII.; HENRY IV. EMPEROR.

HINCMAR, ARCHBISHOP, d. 882, his deposition of Bishop Rotade, viii. 63.

HINDERING KNOWLEDGE. "Why should you hinder people from fighting, if they have a mind to it?"
—*The Scotch Woman*, xviii. 86.

HINDSIGHT. "O, 'tis a vile world! if there is any love or affection to be expected, it must be from a wife; the difficulty is how to choose one."
—*The Prude*, xviii. 183.

HIRELINGS.
"Are, then, these holy instruments of heaven
Infallible? Their ministry indeed
Binds them to the altar, they approach the gods,
But they are mortals still." —*Œdipus*, xvi. 186.

HISTORIAN, a naked truth teller; Historiographer, a smooth story teller, x. 57.

HISTORIANS FALSIFY, philosophers only err, viii. 334.

HISTORIANS AND THEIR HEROES. "The business of a historian is to record, not to flatter; and the only way to oblige mankind to speak well of us, is to contribute all that lies in our power to their happiness and welfare."
—*Charles XII. of Sweden*, xx. 10.

HISTORICAL FABLES, xxxvii. 257.

—— Problem respecting the execution of Joan of Arc, xli. 19.

—— READING. "After having read the descriptions of three of four thousand battles, and the substance of some hundreds of treaties, I do not find myself one jot wiser than when I began, because from them I learn nothing but events."

> —*Observations on History*, xxxvii. 265.

—— TALES. "This has been related by many historians, and cannot be denied without overturning the very foundations of history; but it is equally certain that we cannot give credit to it without overturning the very foundations of reason."

> —*General History*, xxiv. 298.

—— "truth, especially in the ancient stories, diminishes as investigation probes into it," xiv. 132.

HISTORIES, plagarisms and other offenses in, x. 87.

HISTORY VERSUS FABLE, viii. 321.

—— the point of view from which it should be considered xxx. 133; is little else than a long succession of useless cruelties, 135.

—— the study of, what it ought to do for us, xxxvi. 257, 266.

—— Additions to "Ancient and Modern," xxix. xxx. Supplementary notes.

History of Louis XIV. "In this history we confine ourselves to what is deserving of the attention of all ages, what paints the genius and manners of mankind, contributes to instruction, and prompts to the love of virtue, of the arts, and of our country."

> —*Age of Louis XIV.*, xxii. 11.

HOBBES, 1588-1679, not an atheist, viii. 98; would have hanged the man who introduced a God into the Constitution, ix. 240; xxxv. 274.

HOCHSTADT, BATTLE OF, also known as Blenheim, xxiii. 30.

HOLLAND IN THE SEVENTEENTH CENTURY, xxix. 57; its commerce, Calvinism and wars; John of Barneveldt, 62; Grotius, 63.

—— conquest of, by Louis XIV., xxii. 149.

——primitive simplicity of its people under William the Silent, xxvii. 304.

——a custom in, *Essays*, xxxvii. 68.

HOLY DAYS, their effect on national life, ix. 42.

——Ghost, double or single procession of the; how the Nicene creed was made up, xxiv. 127.

——Office, history of the. See INQUISITION.

——Oil, the, made in heaven, note xl. 49.

——See, its return from Avignon to Rome in the Fourteenth century after an absence of seventy-two years, xxv. 237.

HOME.

"Where'er the mind with ease and pleasure dwells,
There is our home, and there our native land."
—*Mahomet*, xvl. 21.

HOMER'S ILIAD, not ridiculous to Greeks, Pope's admission, viii. 251; as a theologian, ix. 311; his ocean was only the Nile, x. 12.

HONEST AND STRONG.

"We are corrupted; but one upright man
May save the state." —*Catiline*, xvii. 241.

HONEYMOONS TAXED BY THE BISHOP, xiv. 65.

HONOR. "Honor is the first of laws,
Let me observe it." —*Œdipus*, xvi. 176.

HONORABLE POVERTY. "Poverty is not intolerable, but contempt is; I am satisfied to be in want, but I would not have it known."
—*The Scotch Woman*, xviii. 18.

HONORS TO MERIT. "The English honor and reward superior talents of every kind. Writers, scientists and artists are Members of Parliament, ambassadors, ministers of state; riches are heaped upon them while they live, and monuments erected to them after their death." —*Preface to Zaïre*, xix. 10.

HOPE.

"All may be well; that hope can man sustain,
All now is well; 'tis an illusion vain."
—*The Lisbon Earthquake*, xxxvi. 18.

HOT-HEADEDNESS.

> "He's ardent and impetuous, and prone
> Sometimes to serve the gods, sometimes offend.
> The world has many characters like his,
> Made up of passion and religious zeal;
> With headlong passion tenderness they mix
> They oft repent, and all things undertake."
>
> —*Olympia*, xv. 113.

HOUSE OF COMMONS, the English, and power of the people, ix. 292.

"HUDIBRAS," Butler's ridicule of the Puritans, vi. 291.

HUGO, VICTOR, Oration on Voltaire, i. 44.

HUGUENOTS, their virtues and political failings, xxi. 113; half a million driven from France, carrying arts and industries with them, 129; persecution of those who returned to France, 131; rise of fanatical sects, 132.

HUMAN NATURE good at bottom, even in the Dark and Middle Ages, xxx. 141.

—— PROGRESS. "It is not in the nature of man to desire what he does not know. He required not only a prodigious space of time, but also a number of lucky circumstances for raising himself above the level of mere animal life."   —*General History*, xxiv. 16.

—— sacrifices in all religions, x. 135.

HUMANITY.

> "Is there a man from human error free?
> Is there a King without some human weakness?"
>
> —*Brutus*, xv. 244.

HUME, DAVID, 1711-1776, his weighty argument, xii. 263.

HUMILIATION.   "Wanders unknown,

> Unpitied, suffers all the bitter woes
> And cruel scorn that waits on penury;
> Misery like this will bend the firmest soul."
>
> —*Mérope*, xv. 50.

HUMILITY. "Some people will give themselves very humble titles providing they are sure of receiving very proud ones in return."

> —*Titles of Honor*, xxxvii. 205.

HUSBANDRY. "Love, my dear niece, is not always the only thing to be thought of." —*The Prude*, xviii. 165.

HURON, THE, OR PUPIL OF NATURE. See ROMANCES.

HUSS, JOHN, 1369-1415, xxi. 109; ignorance of the people and tyranny of the Church, xxv. 260; good men burned at the stake, 266.

HYPNOTIC Manifestations of the Convulsionaries of 1724, vii. 286.

HYPOCRISY.

"Henceforth let mortals know that there are crimes
Offended heaven never can forgive."
—*Sémiramis*, xvii. 225.

A PHILOSOPHICAL DICTIONARY.

VOL. X. HAPPY—HYPATIA.

H.

HAPPY; the philosopher mistaken who said "Call no man happy until he is dead," x. 5; is man happier than woman? 6.

HEAVEN, the firmament; our illusions, 9; theory that the earth is flat, 11; astronomical absurdities of the Early Fathers, 13; Homer's conception of the upper realm of the gods, 15; Moses as a philosopher and scientist, 19.

HELL, its king, queen, housekeepers and fate-dealers, its royal councillors and three-headed dog, 22; Virgil, Lucretius, Horace, Seneca and Cicero laughed at the fabled inferno, 23; hell not mentioned in the Pentateuch, 24; its revival by Jesus, 25; utility of the doctrine of eternal damnation to some divines, 31, 32; the descent of Jesus into, 33; dicta of Peter and the Early Fathers, 34.

HERESY, the unjust stigma of, 36; the Pagan religions knew nothing of heresy, being concerned with moral conduct, 39; rise of the persecuting spirit in Christianity, 39; persecution creates faction, 44; toleration the surest method of weakening a sect, 45; toleration was never a clerical virtue, 47; the simple and sweet

(End of Philosophical Dictionary.)

I

IDLE SOULS.
> " 'Tis best the mind should be employed,
> Indolence leaves a craving void;
> The soul is like a subtle fire
> Which if not fed must soon expire."
>
> —*To a Princess*, xxxvi. 208.

IDIOMATIC EXPRESSIONS in every language, xxxvii. 10.

IGNATIUS ST., d. 107, martyrdom of, vii. 144.

IGNORANCE, our knowledge ends in, xi. 271.

IGNORANCE.   "My triumphs
> From error's fruitful source incessant flow."
>
> —*Mahomet*, xvi. 63.

—— "In the whirlpool called the world
> Man's through so many errors hurled,
> That it can coxcombs please alone
> By whom it ne'er was rightly known."
>
> —*To Madame De* ...., xxxvi. 218.

IGNORANT PHILOSOPHER, THE, xxv. 219.   See PHILOSO-
PHER, THE IGNORANT.

IMAGES venerated but not worshipped by pagans and in
oriental religions, x. 127.

IMAGINATION.   "The ties of nature
> Are not more strong than those of fantasy."
>
> —*Orphan of China*, xv. 203.

IMMACULATE CONCEPTION OF THE VIRGIN MARY, *by her
mother*, (the doctrine widely misconceived to this
day), xiv. 141.

IMMERSION, BAPTISM BY.
> "One can't but think it somewhat droll,
> Pump water thus should cleanse a soul." vi. 202.

IMMORTALITY, will John Smith still be John Smith when
he is an angel or a denizen of hell? x. 116.

—— Bishop Warburton on the disbelief by the Jews in,
xiii. 73.

IMPERIALISM.   "New empires will demand
New names; we must have one more great, more sacred,
Less liable to change."   —*Cæsar*, xix. 104.

IMPERIOUS CÆSAR.

"But Cæsar is beloved, respected, feared,
The Senate and the people all admire
And court him; statesman, general, magistrate;
In peace revered, and terrible in war;
A thousand ways he charms the multitude."
                            —*Catiline*, xvii. 245.

IMPOSE ON THE PEOPLE, how far should we, xxxvii. 199.

IMPOSSIBILITIES, *i. e.*, miracles, xi. 272.

IMPOSTORS.   "Every bold impostor
May forge new fetters and enslave mankind;
He has a right, it seems, to cheat the world
If he can do it with an air of grandeur."
                            —*Mahomet*, xvi. 41.

IMPRUDENCE.

"The bonds that folly and imprudence knit
Are dangerous; guilt doth sometimes follow close
The steps of innocence; our hearts deceive us,
And love, with all his store of dear delights,
May cost us tears."   —*Mahomet*, xvi. 50.

IMPULSES.

"To feel a passion for a worthy object,
Is not a weakness in us but a virtue."
                            —*Mariamne*, xvi. 241.

INCESTUOUS OFFENSES, xii. 76.

INCIDENTS IN THE LIFE OF VOLTAIRE, i. 15.

INCORRUPTIBLE.   "Thy outrageous virtue
Can serve no purpose but to make thee foes."
                            —*Catiline*, xvii. 268.

INCREDULITY THE FOUNDATION OF ALL KNOWLEDGE, xxxvii. 269.

INDEPENDENCE. "It is with the point of the sword
that diplomas should be signed securing this natural
prerogative," xiv. 155.

INDIA, two thousand five hundred years ago, xxiv. 39;
fables of Pilpay, 39; the game of chess, 40; the custom of suttee, 42; Brahmin religions, sublimity and
superstition, 437; xxix. 134, 173; its learning, cus-

—— how it exterminated a happy community, ix. 302; a satire on its decrees, xxxvii. 190; note, xl. 240.

INQUISITOR, IN THE INFERNO.

"I ne'er was born to doom mankind to die,
Wherefore, I'm broiled for making others fry."
—La Pucelle, xl. 180.

INSIGHT.

"I know thee well, thy virtues and thy frailty;
Know what thou canst and what thou darest not do."
—Catiline, xvii. 285.

—— "He judges not of soldiers by their size."
—Epistle, xxxvi. 252.

INSTINCT, the soul of beasts, xiii. 273.

INSTINCTIVE PERCEPTION OF JUSTICE imparted to us by God, xi. 27.

INSUBORDINATE CHILDREN. "All the crosses and disappointments that make families unhappy, come from undutiful daughters." *—The Prodigal*, xix. 160.

INTEREST IS THE GOD OF MEN, when banded in sects, xiv. 106.

INTOLERANCE. "If you have two religions among you, they will massacre each other; if you have thirty they will live in peace." xiv. 103.

—— "Religion is a dreadful power."
—Mahomet, xvi. 66.

—— "Go and get together as many bawling enthusiasts as you can, and cry out, Impiety! Impiety!"*—Socrates*, xvi. 293; xii. 154. See TOLERATION.

INTROSPECTION.

"Of mercy every mortal stands in need.
If innocence alone could heaven approach,
Who in this temple would adore the gods?"
—Olympia, xv. 118.

INVENTIONS, by the Chinese of antiquity, paper, silk stuffs, porcelain, astronomical instruments, glass, printing, bells, gunpowder, xxiv. 27.

—— of the fourteenth century, xxvi. 42; windmills, clocks,

A PHILOSOPHICAL DICTIONARY.

Vol. X. Continued.

IDEA—INUNDATION.

Idea; ideas, like our hair, can be dressed and cultivated, but not produced at will, x. 104; ideas given us by the Eternal Being, 109; organization of the senses, 110; God the universal principle of all things, 113.

Identity, the body changes, memory remains, 114; difficulties in the doctrine of personal immortality and future punishment, 116.

Idol, idolator, idolatry; no adoration of idols in paganism or Catholicism, 120; the ancient idolatry examined, 121; the images of gods were not the gods, 127; whether the Persians, Sabines, Egyptians, Tartars and Turks have been idolaters, 127; human sacrifices, 135; pure theism of Epictetus and Marcus Aurelius, 137.

Ignatius Loyola, 1491-1566, otherwise St. Inigo the Biscayan, 139; his remarkable life, 140; in contrast with George Fox the Quaker and Count Zinzendorf the Moravian, 142. See Jesuits; Loyola.

Ignorance, most dangerous in critics, reply to the Abbé Francois, 143; Adonai, Melchom, Jehovah, Baal, Bel, Shaddai, Eloi, 146; Newton, 150.

Imagination, the philosophy of, 155; passive and active, 159; its uses in literature and art, 165; imagination of animals, dogs hunt in dreamland, 167; our inability to create an idea or image, 168.

Impious Conception of God, representing a bearded being, 172; judging Him by the creature's standard, 173.

Impost, tax gatherers cursed in Holy Writ, 174; modes of raising money to sustain government, 176.

Impotence, ancient law and witchcraft relating to, 181; Mosaic code does not deal with it, 183; the gospels on divorce, 183; the cases of Henry IV. of Castile, Alfonso of Portugal, and the Marquis de Langeais, 184.

INALIENATION, inalienable domain, 187.

INCEST, 188.

INCUBUS AND SUCCUBUS, cohabitation with devils, 190.

INFINITY, beyond finite ken, 193; infinite power, wisdom, goodness; God can make a stick without two ends, but does not, 199.

INFLUENCE, its actuality and mystery, 199; upon the fœtus, 203.

INITIATION, ancient mysteries, 205; pagan slanders against the Christian mysteries, 211; the accusations by Christian writers, 212.

INNOCENTS, massacre of the, examination of the evidence, 214.

INQUISITION, THE, originated with the Apostles, 218; history of, 220; citations from instructions to Inquisitors authorizing atrocious rulings, 230-235; the Inquisition in Portugal; a powerful machine for increasing the power of priests and the breed of hypocrites, 235.

INSTINCT, something divine, 241.

INTEREST, the prime motive in religion and commerce, 243; the Jansenist and the Dutch merchant, 245.

INTOLERANCE, the damnation of the great and good, Newton, Locke, Milton, Shakespeare, et al., 248.

INUNDATION, an impossible universal, 251.

(End of Philosophical Dictionary.)

J

JACK IN OFFICE.
"It ill becomes a temporary power,
Like thine, to boast of its authority."
—*Catiline*, xvii. 236.

JACOVELLO AND THE ORACLE, xii. 95.

JAEL, the nail she drove into Sisera's head, note, xl. 93.

JAMES II. OF ENGLAND, 1633-1701, befriended as refugee by Louis XIV., xxii. 223. See IRELAND, and STUARTS.

JANSENISM WAS BEGUN IN 1552 by Michael De Bay, xxi. 141; was condemned by Pius V. in 1567, 142; the doc-

her in those heroic times when mankind were wont to decree such honors to their deliverers," xxvi. 35.

—— a French portrayal of her charms, note, xl. 87, 96, 97; historical problem respecting her execution, xli. 19, 55; a letter by Joan, 247; her trial, 252, 262, 280, 281, 287. See THE HENRIADE, xxxviii. 105.

—— Queen of Naples, consented to the murder of her husband, and had three to succeed him, xxv. 231; she was smothered between two beds, 236.

JOB, an Arab Sheik, vi. 13; the Book of, one of the most precious writings that have come down to us from antiquity, x. 314.

JOHN, King of England, 1166-1216, sentenced to death by the peers of France, xxv. 56; hated by the English, 58; subjects himself to the Pope, 59; degradation of being forced to sign the Magna Charta, 65. See ENGLAND, IRELAND.

—— Palæologus VI., 1332-1391, puts out the eyes of his son, xxvi. 90; the rise of Tamerlane, 92, 103, 111. See TAMERLANE.

JOHNNY, Story of. See ROMANCES.

JOINVILLE, SIEUR DE, 1224-1317, a chronicler of doubtful tales, xxv. 139.

JOKERS, their minds usually incorrect and superficial, xiv. 16.

JOSEPH, EMPEROR, of Germany, 1678-1711, xxiii. 57; death of, 92.

JOSEPHUS, 37-95, his silence upon the massacre of the innocents, the crucifixion, and other matters, vii. 106.

JOURNALISM. "He is my puffer, and can scatter reports about town for me that may be serviceable."
                                        —The Prude, xviii. 196.

JOUSTS AND TOURNAMENTS, xxx. 25.

JOYS OF LIFE.
          " A man must think, or else the brute
            May his superior worth dispute;
            A man must love, for were it not
            For love, most hard would be his lot."
              —The Requisites to Happiness, xxxvi. 267.

JUDAS, the church's verdict on, vii. 33; his suicide a greater sin than his betrayal of Jesus, vii. 33.

—— MACCABAEUS, d. 160 B. C.; his glorious struggles, xiv. 87. "Every man should obey the natural and eternal laws which God has given him." xiv. 88.

JUDICIAL MURDERS, fatal legal blunders, viii. 18.

——   " Those who dare not fight
May screen their guilt beneath the mask of justice
And call the murder legal punishment."
                                        —*Mahomet*, xvi. 45.

JUDICIOUS JUDGMENT.
      "Justice extreme is height of injury,
      We must not always hearken to the voice
      Of rigor."   —*Œdipus*, xvi. 176.

JUDITH AND HOLOFERNES, note, xl. 277.

JULIAN, EMPEROR, 331-363, the so-called Apostate, v. 290; St. Gregory Nazianzen reproaches him for having worn too long a beard; so far from being a persecutor he sought to extirpate persecution and intolerance, 294; x. 76; what he said of the Christians, xiv. 287.

JULIUS II., POPE, 1441-1513, and the League of Cambray, xxvi. 226-241.

JUST AND UNJUST. "Who has given us the perception of just and unjust? God, who gave us a brain and a heart." xi. 27.

JUSTICE.
      " Interest may be the god of Mahomet,
          But mine is Justice."   —*Mahomet*, xvi. 42.

—— AND TRUTH.
      " In earlier days, by vice and crime unstained,
      Justice and Truth, two naked sisters reigned,
      But long since fled, as everyone can tell,
      Justice to heaven, Truth into a well." viii. 132.

JUSTIN MARTYR, vii. 125.

A PHILOSOPHICAL DICTIONARY.

Vol. X. Continued.

JEHOVAH—JOB.

Vol. XI.

JOSEPH—JUSTICE.

JUSTICE, excessive punishments for venial offences, 30; examination of the case of the Verron family, presumptions in their favor and against them, 31; criticisms on the administration of law, 48.

(End of Philosophical Dictionary.)

K

KEPLER, JOHANN, 1571-1630, astronomical discoveries, xxviii. 234.

KINDNESS WINS. "The eyes of friendship seldom are deceived." —*Orestes*, xvii. 118.

KINDRED.

" The ties of blood, and all their boasted power
Are mere delusions. What are nature's bonds?
Nothing but habit, the mere force of custom."
—*Mahomet*, xvi. 63.

KING, A GOOD.

" By right of conquest, and of birth, a King;
In various sufferings resolute and brave,
Faction he quelled; he conquered and forgave.
He taught those realms he conquered to obey,
And made his subjects happy by his sway."
—*The Henriade (Henry IV.)* xxxviii. 9.

KINGLY SIMPLICITY.

" Superior even to the rank he bore,
He was a King who * * * disdained
All irksome pomp, and never would permit
An idle train of slaves to march before him.
Amid his happy subjects fearless still,
And still unguarded lived in peace and safety,
And thought his people's love his best defence."
—*Œdipus*, xvi. 185.

KINGLY WEALTH. "With money we get soldiers, and with soldiers we steal money." xii. 9.

KINGSHIP.

" How very seldom they deserve a crown
Who are born to wear it." —*Brutus*, xv. 264.

A PHILOSOPHICAL DICTIONARY.

VOL. X.—CONTINUED.

KING—KISS.

        (End of Philosophical Dictionary.)

L

LABYRINTH, A. "A labyrinth of fatality and free-will, in which all ages have been bewildered, and where man has no clue to direct his steps." xxi. 141.

LA CHAISE, PÉRE, 1624-1709, governor of Louis XIV.'s conscience, xxi. 161.

LADIES OF THE BEDCHAMBER, how they came to be substituted for Maids of Honor, xxiii. 172.

LADIES' MAN. "His eternal clack teases me to death."
—*The Prude*, xviii. 214.

LA FONTAINE, 1621-1695, xxx. 104; xxxvi. 66; his style, xxxvii. 109; xxxviii. 284.

LAND OF PROMISE, promised more butter than bread, xi. 10.

LANFRANC, ARCHBISHOP, 1005-1089, his view of the sacred body and blood in the Eucharist, xxiv. 295.

LANGEAIS, M. DE, his unfortunate Parliamentary experience, xiv. 206.

LARGE-HEARTED.
"'Tis merit others' merit thus to own,
To a true genius envy is unknown."
—*Envy*, xxxvi. 187.

LA ROCHEFOUCAULD, DUKE DE, 1613-1680, xxxviii. 299.

LATIN PRAYERS, why introduced among people who did not understand them, xxiv. 135.

LAUD, ARCHBISHOP, 1573-1645, executed for treason, xxviii. 277.

LAUZUN, DUC DE MONTPENSIER for a day imprisoned by Louis XIV., xxiii. 158, 175.

LA VALLIERE, MADEMOISELLE, and Louis XIV., xxiii. 123, 132, 149, 153, 155.

LAW, JOHN, 1671-1729, his French financial scheme a sham, xiii. 48; xxxvii. 211.

LAW OF LOVE.
"This is the law divine, the heavens above
Explained man's duty when they bade to love."
—*The Nature of Virtue*, xxxvi. 189.

Or insolent; he is your equal still,
Or still your foe, because inferior to you;
He cannot bear the lustre of high fortune,
In all the service you have done him, sees
Naught but the injury you have power to do."

—*Brutus*, xv. 259.

LEYDEN, defence of, 1574-1575, by the Dutch against the
Spanish, xxvii. 294.

LIBERTY, i. 289.

—— of conscience, a German parable, vii. 240.

—— love of, in England, ix. 291.

—— the English were the first nation in the world in,
xxviii. 19.

LIES, a clear head required to perceive their nature and
uses, xiv. 254.

LIFE.

"Of Solomon the judgment sage you've heard,
Like oracle, men listened to his word;
Console yourself—wisdom in turn will reign,
We sin in youth, when old, we grace obtain."

—*La Pucelle*, xli. 65.

——   "Live with ease, and die
When life grows burdensome."

—*Orphan of China*, xv. 233.

—— VOWS IN MARRIAGE. "It is very (funny) to
promise, for a whole life, that which no man can certainly ensure from night to morning!" xiv. 180.

LIGHT DENIED.

"To nature we apply for truth in vain,
God should His will to human kind explain."

—*The Lisbon Earthquake*, xxxvi. 15.

LIMBO, purgatory, "the paradise of fools," xii. 125.

LISBON, the earthquake of, xxxvi. 8.

LITERARY MAN, THE, a flying fish; if he rises the birds
devour him; if he dives, the fishes eat him, xi. 119.

LOBKOVITZ, PRINCE, his victory at Prague, "War of 1741,"
xxxiii. 93.

LOCALITY MAKES INNOCENCE CRIMINAL, xii. 73.

149; massacre of the two chief statesmen of Holland, 159; Louis now the only strong King in Europe, 164; Holland evacuated, 173; re-conquest of Franche-Comté, 175; glorious campaign and death of Turenne, 175; battles and victories, the Peace of Nimeguen, 1678, 189.

Capture of Strasburg, bombarding of Algiers, submission of the Genoese, 206; Louis sends an embassy to Siam, 218; Pope Innocent XI. blames Louis for joining with Turks against Christians, 219; Louis took Avignon from the Pope and prepared to move against the Pope's friend the German Emperor, 223. James II. of England, dethroned by the revolution of 1688, is protected by Louis, 223; battle of the Boyne won by William III. and the Protestants over James II. and his French allies, 233; France checked on sea and land, 238; death of James II., the ill-fated Stuarts, 240. Affairs in Europe, 241; enemies of Louis, 241; battle of Philippsburg, 243; burning of the Palatinate, 250, 263. France still subduing her foes, 264; treaty with Savoy, the Peace of Ryswick, 267; Louis crippled financially, makes some restrictions of territory, 269; noble character and rule of Leopold of Lorraine, 270; Europe troubled by the rise of two men, the most extraordinary the world ever produced, Peter the Great and Charles XII. of Sweden, 275; Charles II. of Spain, character and death of, and effects of his political testament, 278, 285; great stroke of policy by which Louis XIV. acquired power over the Spanish monarchy and secured his dynasty, 288; he refuses to recognize the sovereign title of the son of James II. of England, 291; death of William III., 294; character of, 295; succession of Queen Anne to the English throne, 296; at sixty years of age Louis faces serious troubles at home and abroad, 299.

Volume XXIII.

The war of 1701, xxiii. 5; Prince Eugene, his family and early career, 6; captures Marshal Villeroi at

ordered, ailing in body, depressed in mind, having lost public respect, 204; betting on the King's death, 205; a dignified departure, 207; his character, 208.

Louis gives a King's advice to Kings in the memorial penned by his own hand, 211; counsels to his grandson, Philip V. of Spain, 215; Louis not brilliant, but just and noble, 219; characteristics of Louis XIV., 219; his children, 228, 298.

As King, Louis encouraged his people to petition him, wrote despatches himself, and was a hard worker, 230; he remitted arrears of taxes, improved the roads, and encouraged commerce, 232; established the East and West India Companies, greatly benefitting trade, 234; encouraged marriage and large families, and manufactures of every kind, 236; Louis had a fine taste for architecture, landscape gardening, sculpture, and elegant palaces, 239; entrance to the Louvre, Hotel des Invalides, college of St. Cyr, the observatory, and the canal of Languedoc, monuments of his reign, 242; improved legislation, 243; abolished duels, 244; gave uniforms to the troops, in which his example was followed by all nations, 245; established the use of bayonets, and improved the management of artillery, 246; Louis first started the practice of military manœuvers and sham battles in time of peace, 248; he built a navy, and established colonies, 251; his influence upon the nation, 254; on manners, 258; the finances under Colbert, 261-272; multiplication of industries, 273; progress of the sciences, 277-286; the arts in the time of Louis XIV., 286; greater advances made by England than by France, 287; Milton, Waller, Earl of Dorset, Earl of Roscommon, Duke of Buckingham, Dryden, Pope, Addison, Swift, as poets, 289; English scholars, theologians, philosophers, 291; Leibnitz, Boerhaave, and Italian philosophers, 296; the children of Louis XIV. natural and legitimate, 298; celebrated artists, Poussin, Le Sueur, Lebrun, Claude Lorraine, Watteau, and others.

Fired with this earthly paradise his lot
What's said at night, next morn may be forgot."
—*La Pucelle*, xl. 40.

LOVING KINDNESS. "A God of mercy
Can never hate, can never persecute,
A heart so just, so brave, so good."
—*Zaïre*, xix. 68.

LOYALTY. "When our equals lag
Beneath the stroke of censure, we should act
With caution, and in them respect ourselves."
—*Catiline*, xvii. 273.

LOYOLA, IGNATIUS, 1491-1566, his wonderful life and character, x. 138; the Jesuit founder compared with George Fox and Count Zinzendorf, 142; romance of his life, xxvii. 141; power of the Jesuits, 144; note, xl. 129. See JESUITS.

LUCK, good or bad, in numbers, xii. 60; the "number of the beast," 63.

—— " Fortune doth often reach
What wisdom cannot." —*Mérope*, xv. 74.

—— IN LOVE. "I triumph in thy weakness,
And bless for once the lucky power of love."
—*Amelia*, xvi. 110.

LUCRETIUS, B. C. 50, AND POSIDONIUS. See DIALOGUES. His imaginary retort upon the Cardinal, xxxvii. 48.

LUCULLUS, B. C. 110-58, AND LACTANTIUS, xii. 83.

LULLI, JEAN BAPTISTE, 1633-1687, composer, xxiii. 152.

LUST, gaming and luxury prevail in proportion as the church grows large and powerful, xiv. 160.

LUTHER, 1483-1546, AND ZUINGLIUS, xxvii. 58; the former a vulgar demagogue, 63; influences at work in his day, 65; tenets of their religion, 70; Lutheranism in Sweden, Denmark, Germany, 72; atrocities, 73; Luther grants a divorce, 75.

—— AND CALVIN. Were they to return to the world they would make no more noise than the Scotists and Thomists. The reason is they would appear in an

M

age when men begin to be enlightened, xxxvii. 228; xxx. 69, 77.

Luxembourg, Marshal, 1628-1695, xxii. 252, 257.

LUXURY.

> "Know luxury which destroys a state
> That's poor, enriches one that's great."
> —*The Man of the World,* xxxvi. 171.

—— and Commerce, xxxvii. 211, 216.

A PHILOSOPHICAL DICTIONARY.

VOL. XI.—Continued.

LAUGHTER—LUXURY.

Laughter, the greatest enjoyments are serious, xi. 58; smiles may be malicious, 59.

Law, natural; the obvious rights of property, 60; Jean Jacques Rousseau "ill-conditioned," a sneerer at what the universal sense of mankind holds valuable and sacred, "a thoroughly unsocial animal," 61; bad men in power, and destructive forces in nature, do not prove the failure of natural law, which works beneficently in the main, 63.

—— the Salic; women have not reigned in France because the Scriptures say that lilies neither toil nor spin, 65; examination of, 68-77.

—— of fundamental laws, 66; Christian communism, 67.

—— civil and ecclesiastical, suggestions for the better administration of justice, 77.

Laws, advisability of burning existing statutes and making fewer laws that would work well, speedily, and economically, 79; the Roman code; the French and English, 79; the laws of China, 84; republics and monarchies among animals, fowls and insects, 87; natural law on a desert island, 91; Tamerlane as a law maker, 99; criticisms of Montesquieu's "Spirit of Laws," 100-108.

Lent, taxing meat in, 108; the Church dieting the poor, 109; origin of the fast, in Egypt or in dyspepsia? 111.

Leprosy and smallpox, speculations on their origin, 112.

MIGHT OF RIGHT.
"That right which firm, exalted spirits claim
O'er vulgar minds." —*Mahomet*, xvi. 41.

MINISTRY. "A holy priest
Shall visit thee, and open the fair book
Of wisdom, clear thy mind's obstructed sight,
And give thee liberty and life."
—*Zaïre*, xix. 55.

MIRABAUD'S SYSTEM OF NATURE, ix. 76; 235.

MIRACLE, a violation of inviolable law, xi. 272.

MIRACLE-WORKERS in modern times, their exhibits of
crutch and truss trophies, as in the old pagan days,
ix. 27.

MIRACULOUS BABYHOOD OF ZOROASTER, xiv. 303.

MIRANDOLA, PICO DE LA, 1463-1494, a royal prodigy of learning, xxvi. 203; knew twenty-two languages at eighteen,
and renounced his principality, 1494, 204.

MIRROR.
"If you're so fond of virtue, 'twould become you
To know and practice it." —*Alzire*, xvii. 45.

MIRTH.
"Heart-easing mirth inhabits there,
Mirth, who in repartee delights,
Whose satire pleases, never bites."
—*To a Countess*, xxxvi. 236.

MISERY UNMANS. "The wretched soon unite, and
soon divide." —*Orestes*, xvii. 111.

MISFORTUNE.
"The serious lessons which misfortune brings
Are needful often, and of use to Kings."
—*The Henriade*, xxxviii. 50.

MISGOVERNMENT.
"Thus, by my people still oppressed, I see
Justice give way to faction, interest still,
The arbiter of fate, sells needy virtue
To powerful guilt; the weak must to the strong
For ever yield." —*Mérope*, xv. 34.

MISSIONS TO HEATHEN, "Know that we Christians alone on

the earth are in the right and that we ought to be masters everywhere," xiv. 111.

MISSIONARIES, futility of sending them to disturb the Chinese, vii. 94.

MOB POPULARITY usually implies inferiority of merit, xiv. 58.

MODELS. "In this world one is rarely what he ought to be."   —*Letters*, xxxviii. 193.

MOGUL, THE, xxx. 264; astronomy and astrology in India, xxx. 264.

MOLE AND AN ANT DISCUSS ARCHITECTURE LIKE SKILLED CLERICS, ix. 252.

MOLIÈRE, JEAN BAPTISTE, 1622-1672, xxiii. 137; xxx. 102; xxxvi. 67; xxxviii. 292.

—— and Scarron compared, vi. 291.

MOLINA, 1535-1600, the Jesuit, explained the operations of God's mind.   —*Jansenism*, xxi. 143.

MOLINOS, MICHAEL, 1640-1697, founder of the Quietist sect, xxi. 187.

MOLOCH, the burning idol into which Jewish children were cast to death, xiv. 113.

MONARCHIES, why they prevail, viii. 10.

MONARCHY.
> "Monarchy so oft admired, so oft
> Detested by us, is the best or worst
> Of human governments; a tyrant King
> Will make it dreadful, and a good, divine."
>   —*Brutus*, xv. 280.

MONEY. "In the age we live in everything may be had of everybody but money."   —*The Prude*, xviii. 166.

—— historians prone to be ignorant in their valuation of money in ancient times, xxiv. 25.

—— and the Revenues of Kings, xxxvii. 219.

—— making. Invention of the art of making money by Purgatory, xiii. 30.

—— MARKET. "The devil is certainly at the bottom of this business."   —*Nanine*, xviii. 140.

MONKS AS SLAVE OWNERS, vii. 183.

—— Emperor Constantine Copronymus, in eighth century, styled the monks abominable wretches, xxiv. 93.

—— likened to chicken-killing weasels, xiii. 221.

—— AND NUNS. "There are about seven thousand houses for monks and more than nine hundred convents for women belonging to the Franciscans; an intolerable nuisance where there is an evident decrease of the human species," xxvii. 138.

MONKEYS AND MEN, alike in levity of ideas, the talent of imitation, and inconstancy, xi. 88.

MONOPOLIES, COMMERCIAL. "When commerce is in a few hands, some people make prodigious fortunes, while the greater number remain poor; but when commerce is more widely diffused, wealth becomes general and great fortunes are rare," xxxvii. 19.

"MONSTERS who need superstitions, just as the gizzard of a raven needs carrion," xiv. 103.

MONTAIGNE, MICHEL EYQUEM, 1533-1592, on cannibalism, vii. 15; on kissing, xi. 58; man's duality, xxi. 217, 246; his style neither pure, correct, nor noble, xxxvii. 13.

MONTESPAN, MADAME DE, 1641-1707, note, xli. 107. See "AGE OF LOUIS XIV."

MONTESQUIEU'S "SPIRIT OF LAWS," 1748, viii. 272; his mistaken view of early Christianity, 273; xi. 100; untrustworthy on the slavery question, xiii. 219; xxxviii. 292. See "SPIRIT OF LAWS."

MONTEZUMA, Emperor of Mexico, 1471. See CORTES.

MONTMORENCY, DUKE OF, the most amiable nobleman in France, 1631, xxviii. 193.

MOONSHINE.

"The moon's pale course spoke midnight near at hand, The hour for bliss, which lovers understand."
—La Pucelle, xl. 37.

"The banquet ended, mirth and jest went round; Blind to their own, their neighbors' faults were found."
—La Pucelle, xl. 39.

A PHILOSOPHICAL DICTIONARY.

VOL. XI.—Continued.

MADNESS—MOUNTAIN.

MADNESS, is the immortal soul subject to mortal ailments?
159.

MAGIC, spirit-resurrectionists work not for philosophers,
164; their art a very ancient one, but their greatest
adepts never come back, 164.

MALADY, medicine, the candid physician and his bewildered
royal patient, 166.

MAN, one-third of his life spent in sleep, 170; different
races of, 174; Munchausen stories told by Jerome
and Augustine, as pious facts, 175; is man born
wicked? 181; in a state of nature, 184; operation of
God on man, 188-194.

MARRIAGE CONTRACT, THE, 197; marriages with heretics,
dicta of Augustine and Pope Benedict IV., 198; French
law of, 201.

MARY MAGDALEN, her life poetized, 205; but Mary was
really not a Marchioness nor Lazarus, her brother,
Count of Bethany, 206.

MARTYRS, lives of the, 213-226.

MASS, its beginnings and growth, 229; Acts of John, tells
of the mass dance, quoted by the Second Council of
Nice, 232.

MASSACRES on account of religion, 236.

MASTER, the philosophy of mastership, 236; an Indian
fable, 238.

MATTER, motion, mind; we know little of either, 242.

MEETINGS, public, 247.

MESSIAH, a clerical review of the claims of false Messiahs, 249.

METAMORPHOSIS among the gods, 268.

METAPHYSICS, the romance of the mind, 269.

MIND, limits of the human, does not even know itself,
271.

NARROW MINDS. "Everything great and noble is sure to be attacked by narrow minds." xxii. 90.

NATIONAL DEBTS. "A state which is indebted only to itself can never be impoverished, and even debts are a spur to industry." xxxvii. 225.

NATURE, necessity, freedom, ix. 75.

—— "How deeply simple nature delights me!" xv. 17.

NATURAL LAW, dialogue on, xi. 60; xii. 4, 48.

NAVEL OF JESUS, worshipped in Notre Dame for ages, thrown away by the Bishop of Chalons in 1702, xxi. 106.

NEBUCHADNEZZAR, note, xl. 169.

NEGLECT.

"Oft the soldier, honored in the field,
In courts neglected lies, and is forgotten."
—*Sémiramis*, xvii. 151.

NEMESIS.   "Fortune oft
Deserts us; from the silence of oblivion
Sometimes a secret may spring forth, and heaven
By slow and solemn steps, may bring down vengeance."
—*Mérope*, xv. 40.

NEW FAITH APOSTLES. "My God! what an odd mixture it is! how strangely the old gentleman jumbles his ideas together!"   —*The Prodigal*, xix. 153.

NEW FORMS.

"He bore the pastoral crozier in his hand,
Which was in ancient times the Augur's wand."
—*La Pucelle*, xl. 44.

NESTORIUS, his pious method of putting down heretics, x. 48.

NEWTON, SIR ISAAC, 1642-1727, his theory of attraction, vii. 210; even he had his superstitions, ix. 29; x. 150; xxiii. 291; xxxvi. 74, 299; xxxvii. 164.

—— sketch of his system of philosophy, and that of Descartes, xxxvii. 164, 172.

NICE, The Second Council of, 786; its approval of image worship, xxiv. 125. See COUNCILS.

NITRE-WATER as a means of prolonging life, xiii. 39.

A PHILOSOPHICAL DICTIONARY.

VOL. XII.

A PHILOSOPHICAL DICTIONARY.

VOL. XII.—Continued

OCCULT—OVID.

P

on man, xi. 186; he was the chief of French satirists, of whom Desprèaux was the second, xxi. 151; he created French "style," xiv. 5; remarks on his "Thoughts," xxi. 212; philosophy, 214; Mystery, 215; contradictions, 217; faith or reason, 219; life, 221; Jews, 222; self-love, 226; wit, 244; poetry, 255; liveries, 261; xxxviii. 296.

PASSION.
> "Howe'er the soul may act which virtue guides,
> Its secret motions, nature's children still
> Must force their way; they will not be subdued,
> But in the folds and windings of the heart
> Lurk still, and rush upon us; hid in fires
> We thought extinguished, from their ashes rise."
> —*Œdipus*, xvi. 162.

PASTOR, THE GOOD.   "In solitude
> Obscure he lives; his holy ministry
> Engrosses all his care; is always seen
> Within the temple, never at the court."
> —*Sémiramis*, xvii. 151.

PATERNITY, HAS GOD? vi. 20.
—— "I was born to be an unfortunate father."
> —*The Prodigal*, xix. 147.

PATHS OF LOVE. "Love a man to hell may guide."
> —*The Padlock*, xxxvi. 176.

PATIENCE. "Time softens all things."
> —*Cæsar*, xix. 102.

—— PAYS.
> "Here's your lawyer, sir,"
> "O let him wait."   —*Nanine*, xviii. 135.

PATKUL, Russian soldier and statesman, treacherously murdered by Charles XII. of Sweden, xx. 29, 119; his terrible death, 131; see xxxiv. 172.

PATRIOT, THE.
> "A true republican has neither son,
> Father, nor brother, but the commonweal
> His gods, the laws, his virtue, and his country."
> —*Cæsar*, xix. 119.

PATRIOTISM.
>"All that I wish is but to save my country,
>And if I can be useful to mankind
>This is the ambition I would satisfy."
>
>—*Œdipus*, xvi. 168.

PAUL, ST., his philosophy betrays the influence of Plato, x. 55; his personal appearance, vii. 134.

PAY, IS HUMILITY A VIRTUE, AND DOES IT? x. 101.

PEACEMAKERS, THE, who prevent litigation in Holland, xxxvii. 68.

PEDANTRY. "Those useless and unsociable scholars, who neglect the study of their own tongue to acquire an imperfect knowledge of ancient languages."
>—*Essays*, xxxvii. 7.

PEDIGREE. "We should always keep in mind that no family on earth knows its founder, and, consequently, that no nation knows its origin." xxxiv. 20.

PENALTIES INFLICTED by the Church only take effect in some other world, xiii. 127.

PENATES, the little divinities that preside over the parts of our bodies, xiv. 142.

PENN, WILLIAM, 1644-1718, the Quaker; his code for his Quaker colony more humane and tolerant than the laws given to the colony in Carolina by Locke, and those of Plato, vii. 165, 167. See QUAKERS, DUNKERS.

"PENNSYLVANIANS" not Christians, vi. 47. See QUAKERS. Penn's colony alone among white Christians renounced the slave trade, xiii. 216.

PENTATEUCH known only to the Jews, xii. 21; its authenticity questioned, 26.

PEPIN, the first anointed sovereign in Europe, eighth century, xxiv. 86; the anointing of, xxix. 213.

PERFECTION. "In every art there is a point beyond which we never can advance; we are shut up within the limits of our talents; we see perfection lying beyond us and only make impotent endeavors to attain to it."   —*Preface to Mariamne*, xix. 238.

PERIL. "Danger has taught me wisdom."
—Mariamne, xvi. 223.

PERIL AT THE HELM.
> " Like an unskilful pilot
> He sets up every sail for every wind,
> But still knows not which way the tempest comes,
> Or whither it may drive him."
—Catiline, xvii. 242.

PERPETUA, saint and martyr, xi. 219.

PERRAULT, CLAUDE, 1613-1688, architect of the Louvre, xxiii. 242.

PERSECUTION BEGETS VINDICTIVENESS among saints, x. 44.

PERSECUTION.
> " Fanatic Demon is his horrid name,
> Religion's son, but rebel in her cause,
> He tears her bosom and disdains her laws."
—The Henriade, xxxviii. 73.

PERSIA, its ingenious people, xxiv. 43; its imperial sway before the time of Alexander, 45; fall of its religion, 57.

—— in the sixteenth century, manners and customs, xxvii. 249.

—— in the seventeenth century, xxix. 121; the revolution and its atrocities, 127; the Mogul, 129.

"PERSIAN LETTERS, THE," vii. 263.

PERSONAL IMMORTALITY. If we are changed, can we still be ourselves? x. 116.

PERU, CONQUEST OF, by Pizarro and d'Almagro, private adventurers, xxvii. 218; greatness and cruelty, 222.

PETER, ST., the first Pope, claimed no kingdom but that of heaven, and died a poor man; his successors claimed the earth and left it in the odor of worldly wealth, xiii. 157.

PETER THE HERMIT, 1115. See CRUSADES, xxv. 83.

PETER THE GREAT, 1672-1725; his mighty genius, xx. 33; how he created the Russian Empire; the building of St. Petersburg, 41; he civilized his subjects and yet himself remained a barbarian, 115.

—— "The Russian Empire," xxxiv.-xxxv.; his ancestors, xxxiv. 65; Michael Romanoff, Czar, succeeded,
in 1645, by his son Alexis Michaelovitch, 69; who was
followed, in 1677, by his son Feodor, 72; who nomi-
nated his younger brother, Peter, then ten years old,
as his successor, 74, excluding John, the elder brother,
who had infirmities. On Feodor's death, in 1682, his
sister Sophia fomented a revolt among the Strelitzes,
hoping to attain the throne, 75; terrible barbarities
perpetrated, 77; John and Peter are proclaimed joint
sovereigns, with Sophia as co-regent, 79.

Virtual sovereignty of Sophia, 80; extraordinary
quarrel about religion; Sophia's cruelty, 83; Prince
Golitzin, state minister, 84; Peter, age seventeen, aims
at supreme command, 87; he puts down a conspiracy
against his life, inflicts barbarous punishments, and
banishes John and Sophia, in 1689, 88.

Personal appearance of Peter, his neglected education, early marriage, peculiarities of temperament, 89;
determination to see the world, and introduce the arts
of civilization into his country, 91; raises an army, 95;
treaty with China, 97; conquest of Azov, 101; his travels, 1697, 108; affairs in Europe, death of Sobieski,
King of Poland, and Charles XI. of Sweden, 110;
Peter as a ship carpenter in Holland, 113; visits England, returns home in a ship given him by King William, 119.

Peter's drastic reforms, 1698, 122; dreadful punishments inflicted on rebellious Strelitzes, more than two
thousand being put to death, 123; reforms the church,
127; the calendar, and the ways of the people, 131;
war with Sweden, 135; defeated at Narva, 140; later
victories; entry into Moscow, 162; affairs in Poland;
gains of Charles XII., 166; the tragedy of the Russian
general Patkul, murdered by Charles XII., 172.

Conflicts between Peter and Charles XII., 179; battle of Poltava, 1709, 191; victory of Peter, 194; triumphant entry into Moscow, 202; his power recognized

by England, 204; notes on Peter's achievements, 215; campaign of the Pruth, 217; war with the Turks, 221. Peter is privately married to Catherine in 1707, having repudiated his first wife, Eudoxia, in 1696, 222; proclaimed the marriage in 1711, 223; his troops in difficulties, 232; Catherine counsels proposals of peace; conclusion of a treaty, under which Peter ceases to be aggressive, 248; solemnization of his marriage with Catherine, 253; marriage of the Czarevitch, his son by Eudoxia, 256; his successful sea fight at Aland, 283; master of Finland, 285; development of the country, 295; his second tour through Europe, 296; his reception in France, 301.

Peter's first wife, Eudoxia, opposes his reforms, xxxv. 11; her son, Alexis, shares her views, 13; Peter's remarkable letters to Alexis, with the reply, 14; Peter's ultimatum, threatening to curse his son, 21, who returns, 1717, to make his submission, but is made a prisoner, and his father's formal Declaration is publicly read, charging Alexis with heinous offence and rebellion, demanding his renunciation of heirship to the throne, which is duly made, and Catherine's son is made Czarevitch, 32; Alexis undergoes a formal trial, and confesses to disloyalty, 45; is condemned to death as a would-be parricide, 47; is seized with convulsions and apoplexy, expiring in the presence of the court, the day after his condemnation, 51; public opinion of the affair, 52; Peter stops other intrigues, 59.

How Peter established modern civilization in his country, 60; education, industries, town building, trade, home and foreign, 66; new legal system and its administration, 73; reforms in the church, 76; forms a ruling synod, 77; he decrees that monks and nuns shall do practical work for the good of the community, 81; causes a burlesque marriage of a court fool, as Pope, to an old widow, with decrepit attendants and other tomfooleries, 84.

Death of Charles XII.; its effect on European affairs,

Brahmins, 277. Confucius, 277. Pythagoras and the Grecian philosophers, 279. Zaleucus, 279. Epicurus, 279. The Stoics, 280. Philosophy is virtue, 282. Æsop, 282. Peace, the offering of philosophy, 283. Questions, 283. Ignorance, 285. An Indian Adventure, 289. A short digression, 292. The Dauphin of France, 293.

PHILOSOPHER'S STONE, THE. "A philosopher who has six thousand francs a year has the philosopher's stone."   —*Letters*, xxxviii. 194.

PHILOSOPHERS DO NOT STIR SEDITION, xiv. 27.

"PHILOSOPHICAL DICTIONARY, A," in ten volumes, v.-xiv. See end of each alphabetical section.

PHOTIUS, 891, a great eunuch bishop, made Patriarch of the Greek Church in 858 after being promoted five times in five days, xxiv. 204; his contempt for the Pope of Rome, 209.

PHYSICIAN, The Candid, and his royal patient, xi. 166.

PIUS II., 1405-1464, upheld the marriage of Popes, vii. 201.

PIZARRO, d. 1541, conqueror of Peru. See PERU.

PLAGUE OF SCHISM, a mania curable only by rational thought, xiii. 175.

PLAIN LIVING.

> " 'Tis nothing but a name,
> A word without a meaning; in the days
> Of our forefathers men respected it."
>   —*Catiline*, xvii. 266.

—— "My mistress, sir, is very rich; if she is not expensive, it is because she hates pomp; she is plainly clad, out of modesty, and eats little, because temperance is prescribed to her."
>   —*The Scotch Woman*, xviii. 15.

PLAIN SPEECH.

> "How do you contrive to be so universally hated?"
> "It is because I have merit."
>   —*The Scotch Woman*, xviii. 6.

PLATO'S DREAM, D. C. 429-347. See ROMANCES. Plato on

That man's the victim of unceasing woe,
And lamentations which inspire my strain
Prove that philosophy is false and vain."
                    —*The Lisbon Earthquake*, xxxvi. 8.

POPES, THE, their powers and offenses, xii. 162; their
perquisites; sliding scale of fees to buy pardon for
crimes against the person, xiv. 62.

—— enjoying luxurious possession, need not worry over
the doubt whether St. Peter founded their throne,
xiv. 190.

—— in Otho's time; accusations against them of immorali-
ties and cruelty, of creating a ten-year-old boy a
bishop; castrating a cardinal, etc., xxiv. 232-240.

—— their quarrels and wars with kings and emperors,
xxiv. xxv.

—— Sixtus V., 1521-1590, "the Ass of Ancona," *The
Henriade*, xxxviii. 60.

—— Stephen III., forges a letter from St. Peter, dating
from heaven, xxiv. 86.

POPE, FRENCH GOVERNMENT AND THE. "It is the maxim
of the French Government to look upon him as a
sacred and enterprising person, whose hands must
sometimes be tied, though they kiss his feet."
                    —*The Age of Louis XIV.*, xxii. 22.

POPES, GREAT AND SMALL. "Ye are but mortals
like ourselves, no more."   —*Alzire*, xvii. 40.

POPULAR AUTHOR. "Everybody abuses me, and gives
me money; I am certainly a cleverer fellow than I
thought I was." —*The Scotch Woman*, xviii. 65.

—— preachers, some good clerics bad men, ix. 25.

—— opinion hard to overcome, xii. 79.

—— RAGE. "The two brothers, John and Cornelius De
Witt, honorable statesmen of Holland, were tortured
and massacred at The Hague by a mad multitude because they had sued for peace when their country was
conquered by Louis XIV. One of them had governed the land for nineteen years with spotless integ-
rity; the other defended it at the risk of his life.

These barbarities are common in all nations, for the
populace is almost everywhere the same." xxii. 159.

POPULATION, migration of superfluous peasantry into the
cities, xiii. 7.

PORTOCARRERO, CARDINAL, influence in Spanish affairs, xxii.
283.

PORTUGAL, Plot against the King of, xxx. 239; punishments
for, 241.

PORTUGUESE NAVIGATORS and Discoverers, xxvi. 183; xxvii.
163.

POSTHUMOUS FAME.
"At length applause true merit shares,
'Tis true, but oft the owner dies
Ere to his worth men ope their eyes." xxxvi. 223.

POTIPHAR'S WIFE CONVICTED by a wise infant in its cradle,
xi. 6.

POTTER'S VESSEL, THE.
"If heaven
Expects obedience, it must give us laws
We can obey." (A pint mug cannot hold a quart.)
—*Orestes*, xvii. 126.

POVERTY, pain, war, and charity, vii. 70; the vow of
monks who forthwith become wealthy, xiii. 8.

—— PIOUS. "I've served the cause of heaven and yet am
wretched." —*Sémiramis*, xvii. 221.

POWER DIVINE.
"A God once dwelt on earth amongst mankind,
Yet vices still lay waste the human mind;
He could not do it, this proud sophist cries,
He could, but He declined it, that replies."
—*The Lisbon Earthquake*, xxxvi. 15.

—— TO GET AND GIVE. "Increase of riches is increase
of happiness." —*The Prodigal*, xix. 157.

PRACTICAL RELIGION.
"I am a simple, plain old man, and here
Worship the gods, adore their justice, live
In humble fear of them, and exercise
The sacred rites of hospitality;

Ye both are welcome to my little cottage,
There to despise with me the pride of kings,
Their pomp and riches; come, my friends, for such
I ever hold the wretched." —*Orestes*, xvii. 86.

PRAGMATIC SANCTION, THE, xxx. 176.

PRAGUE, Battle of, xxx. 179.

—— taken by the French in half an hour; was evacuated
on honorable terms after a siege of five months by
Prince Lobkovitz, "War of 1741," xxxiii. 93.

PRAYER.
" Great God, whose being by Thy works is known,
My last words hear from Thy eternal throne;
If I mistook 'twas while Thy law I sought,
I may have erred, but Thou wast in each thought.
Fearless I look beyond the open grave,
And cannot think the God who being gave
The God whose favors made my bliss o'erflow
Has doomed me, after death, to endless woe."
—*The Law of Nature*, xxxvi. 39.

PRAYERS UNANSWERED.
"The gods
Refuse to hear or answer to our vows,
Their silence shows how much they are offended."
—*Œdipus*, xvi. 170.

PREACHERS seldom denounce popular wars, xiv. 197.

—— "O, stupid mortals, with what ease we teach
Your tongues those things which are beyond our
reach !" —*La Pucelle*, xli. 133.

PREACHING THE GOSPEL of mercy with a sword up one's
sleeve, xiii. 86.

PRECIPITANCY. "Those who go into a convent in
haste, generally live to repent it at leisure."
—*The Prude*, xviii. 165.

PREDESTINATION.
"Wayward fortune
Espoused thy cause, and gave a tyrant power
To scourge mankind."
—*Orphan of China*, xv. 207 ; see CALVINISM.

PRIOR AND BUTLER, English satirical poets, vi. 291, xii. 303.

PRIMITIVE Christianity a fraternity, vii. 159.

PRINCE HENRY THE NAVIGATOR OF PORTUGAL, 1394-1460, xxvii. 165.

PRINCE OF THE HOLY ROMAN EMPIRE, one who has learned what concomitant grace is, and has forgotten it, xiv. 93.

PRINTED LIES, fabulous histories, political testaments, anecdotes, letters, court memoirs, and biographies. The libels on Pope, the English poet, and how he stopped them, xxi. 265; spurious works attributed to Cardinal Richelieu, 285-308.

PRINTER'S INK. "The ease with which a writer may impose on the public and spread abroad the most flagrant . calumnies is unhappily one of the greatest inconveniences attending the noble art of printing."
xxxiv. 13.

PRISCILLIANISTS, their alleged infamous orgies, xiv. 297.

PROCRASTINATION. "Well I know
How sloth deludes us; tempting are her charms
But fatal is their end." —Zaïre, xix. 29.

PRODIGIES, "freaks," monsters; the mystery of birth, xii. 13.

PROGRESS. "We have made greater progress than other people in more than one art and science; perhaps we proceed the faster because we began so late." xxiv. 65.

—— of Nations, recapitulation of the histories, xxx. 247.

—— "Rome but changed her fetters,
And for one king hath found a hundred tyrants."
—Brutus, xv. 250.

PROPERTY, the rights of, xi. 60. Rousseau set down as an anarchistical disturber of the laws of God and man, 61.

PROSY writers prone to criticize poetry they are incapable of writing, xiv. 157.

PROTESTANTISM, persecutions, coercions, and banishments, xxi. 127.

PROUDEST TITLE.
"Conqueror, now assume a nobler title,
Now be thy country's friend and give her peace."
—Brutus, xv. 280.

PROVERBS OF SOLOMON, debased by foolish and harmful passages, xiii. 243.

PROVIDENCE.

"The arm of God, that makes the weakest strong,
Will cherish and support a tender flower
That bends beneath the fury of the storm."
                                —*Zaïre*, xix. 58.

PROVIDENCE BROKERS.

"We must not rest our faith on priests alone;
Even in the sanctuary traitors oft
May lurk unseen, exert their pious arts
To enslave mankind, and bid the destinies
Speak or be silent just as they request them."
                                —*Œdipus*, xvi. 171.

"PROVINCIAL LETTERS" of Pascal. "They were models of eloquence and raillery. The best comedies of Molière have not more wit in them than the first part of those letters, nor the writings of Bossuet more sublimity than the latter."   —*Jansenism*, xxi. 153.

PRUDE, A.

"What a deal one has to go through to be a prude!
Would it not be better after all to fear nothing,
To affect nothing, and be a plain woman of honor?"
                                —*The Prude*, xviii. 225.

PRUDENT. "The prudent men do themselves good, the virtuous one does it to others." xiv. 164.

—— ENTHUSIASM.   "Preserve this happy virtue,
'Twill make thee happy and 'will make thee great."
                                —*Amelia*, xvi. 111.

PRURIENT PRUDERY. "Excess of virtue is disgusting."   —*The Prude*, xviii. 227.

PSALMIST AND POPE.

"David, exempt both from restraint and shame
Could to a hundred beauties tell his flame,
Whilst at the Vatican, the Pope distressed,
Can't without scandal be of one possessed."
                                —*The Law of Nature*, xxxvi. 27.

PSYCHE, the soul of the senses, xiii. 266.

A PHILOSOPHICAL DICTIONARY.

VOL. XII.—Continued.

PARADISE—PURGATORY.

A PHILOSOPHICAL DICTIONARY.

VOL. XIII. PROPERTY—PURGATORY.

PROPHECIES, how fulfilled in the New Testament, 11; those of Zoroaster, Plato, and Confucius, 13; a Dutch prophet explains the Apocalypse, 17; the Early Fathers not Hebrew scholars, 19; Rabbinical interpretation of the "prophesied" virgin birth of Jesus, 21; sad obstinacy of the Jews in rejecting the ingenious perversions of the Church's commentators, 22.

PROPHETS, genuine or make-believe, they mostly came to a sad end; Jeddo eaten by a lion because he had sinned in swallowing a morsel of bread; Jonah temporarily engulfed by a remarkable fish; Habakkuk whirled through the air by a hair of his head; Micaiah boxed on the ear by Zedekiah, and Amos had his teeth extracted by King Amaziah, to prevent him from prophesying, 24; difficulties in understanding the clear explanations of inspired prophecy, 25.

PROVIDENCE, Sister Fessue and a metaphysician discuss the recovery of her sparrow's health as the answer to the nine Ave Marias she had said, 28.

PURGATORY not a doctrine of the primitive church, 36; was at first treated as a heresy, 37; the idea borrowed from the Brahmins, Egyptians and Platonists, 38.

(End of Philosophical Dictionary.)

Q

Q, the celebrated scholar, Ramus, persecuted because he taught a new way of pronouncing this letter, xiv. 139.

QUACKERY OF MIND, the sophistry of transforming abstract ideas into realities, xiii. 260.

QUAKERS, THE, xxxix. 192; their endeavor to found a religious colony of Primitive Christians, vii. 165. See PENN.

QUALITY. "A man whom all the world admires, a man of a million."   —*The Prodigal*, xix. 193.

—— TELLS. "My services are my patrons; the only artifices I make use of; I never was at court in my life."   —*The Prude*, xviii. 173.

QUEEN ANNE OF AUSTRIA's nickname for Cardinal Richelieu, xiii. 225.

—— Elizabeth, 1533-1602, and Mary Stuart, xiii. 196.

QUEENS ISABELLA, ELIZABETH AND MARIA THERESA show that a republic may entrust its government to a woman, xiv. 260.

QUEER WORLD, A. "The world is very strangely governed. An English beggar, become Pope of Rome, bestows Ireland by his own authority, on a man who wants to usurp it. Adrian sends Henry II. a ring as a mark of the investiture of Ireland. If a king had given a ring upon conferring a minor church position, he would have been guilty of sacrilege."

xxv. 35.

QUESNEL, PÉRE, 1634-1719; his Jansenist book, xxi. 160.

QUESTIONS still awaiting answers, xiv. 207.

QUIETISM, one of those extravagant sallies of the imagination and theological subtleties, which would not be remembered but for two illustrious names, Madame Guyon and Archbishop Fénelon, xxi. 179; history of the movement, 180; influence of Madame de Maintenon, 181. See FÉNELON, GUYON, xxx. 305.

QUINAULT, PHILIP, xxiii. 151; xxxvi. 67, 94; xxxviii. 297.

A PHILOSOPHICAL DICTIONARY.

VOL. XIII.—CONTINUED.

QUACK.

QUACK, CHARLATAN. Doctors flourish best in cities; the famous Dumoulin, dying, said he left two great physicians behind him—simple diet and soft water, 39; Doctor Villars, his wonderfully successful prescription for would-be centenarians—water and nitre, 40; quackery in science and literature, 42.

(End of Philosophical Dictionary.)

R

REFORMATION. See LUTHER, HENRY VIII., ENGLAND, SCOTLAND.

REGENCY, THE.
  "Then folly, tinkling loud her bells in hand,
    With lightsome step, tripped over Gallia's land,
    Where to devotion not a soul was prone,
    And every act save penitence was known."
                              —*La Pucelle*, xli. 92.

REGIMEN better than medicine, xii. 197.

RELATIVE EQUALITY.
  "Dost thou not know that the poor worm which
      crawls
    Low on the earth, and the imperial eagle
    That soars to heaven, in the all-seeing eye
    Of their eternal Maker are the same
    And shrink to nothing? Men are equal all,
    From virtue only true distinction springs
    And not from birth."   —*Mahomet*, xvi. 26.

RELEASE. "Who wishes but for death, is sure to find it."
                              —*Amelia*, xvi. 135.

RELICS, Procession of, 1762, the bones of the children
    massacred by Herod, a bit of the Virgin Mary's gown;
    thirty corpses; relics of St. Peter and St. Paul, xxxviii.
    258.

—— of the Cross, the Virgin's milk, her hair, her gown,
    etc., xiv. 18; xii. 46; of the saints, note, xli. 271.

RELIGION IN FRANCE, under the Reformation, xxvii. 119;
    of the Chinese, xxiv. 31.

RELIGION. "We must make use of every expedient to
    promote a good cause; it is the only way to live happy
    here and gain heaven hereafter."
                              —*Socrates*, xvi. 294.

RELIGIOUS AND ECCLESIASTICAL MOVEMENTS, Council of
    Trent, xxi. 67; ecclesiastical affairs of France, 90;
    Calvinism, 107; Jansenism, 141; Quietism, 179; Jews,
    193; Remarks on Pascal's "Thoughts," 212; on Printed
    Lies, 265; xi. 130.

—— assemblies subject to civil law, xiii. 122.

—— confusion in England under Henry VIII., xxvii. 107.

—— fanaticism, assassinations due to, xxx. 233, 239.

—— Orders, The, great men and great work for good due to the monastic system, which is also responsible for much harm in the world, xxvii. 131-150.

RELIGIOUS CONTROVERSY.

" If you are disputants, my friends, pray travel
When you come home again you'll cease to cavil."
　　　　　　　　　　—On Disputation, viii. 130.

—— CRANKERY, evolution of, xiv. 204.

REMEMBRANCE.　　　　" O think
　　　　　On our past loves." —Alzire, xvii. 49.

REMORSE.　　　　" My little dream
　　　Of happiness is o'er, and conscience darts
　　　Its sudden rays on my affrighted soul."
　　　　　　　　　　—Orestes, xvii. 79.

REVERENT ACKNOWLEDGMENT of our ignorance more becoming than derision when we meditate on the occult, xii. 73.

REPUBLIC, A. "Not founded on virtue but on the ambition of every citizen, which checks the ambition of others; on pride restraining pride; and on the desire of ruling, which will not suffer another to rule."
　　　　　　　—Thoughts on Government, xxxvii. 237.

—— or Monarchy, viii. 10.

REPUBLICS, unlike monarchies, do not allow women to share in the government, xiv. 259.

REPUTATION.

" You'll often be betrayed, belied,
　　You ne'er of virtue made parade,
　　To hypocrites no court you've paid."
　　　　　　　　　　—On Calumny, xxxvi. 89.

RESERVE. "You are always repeating truths of some kind or other; but let me tell you, truth is not always agreeable."　　　　　—The Prodigal, xix. 149.

RESPECT, LOYAL. "True philosophers respect princes, but never flatter them."
　　　　　　—Dedication to Queen Caroline, xxxviii. 6.

RIGHTS, POLITICAL.
"Draw from the people's rights your power alone,
Friends of the State."
—*The Henriade*, xxxviii. 68.

RIP VAN WINKLE outdone by the Seven Sleepers of
Ephesus who slept for one hundred and seventy-seven
years, xiii. 222.

RISE OF THE PERSECUTING SPIRIT IN CHRISTIANITY, x. 39.

RIVAL POPES, two, Anacletus, son of a Jew, and Innocent
II., d. 1143, xxiv. 267.

ROCH, ST., note, xl. 185.

ROCHELLE, LA, SIEGE OF. See RICHELIEU.

ROCROI, Condé's victory at, xxii. 41.

ROD, THE. "Calamity, that best of masters."
—*Orphan of China*, xv. 231.

ROLLO THE NORMAN BANDIT, d. 932, xxiv. 172, acquired
Normandy and Brittany and became Christian, established justice among his Danes and Franks, who
became the conquerors of England, xxiv. 174.

ROMAN EMPERORS, THE, note, xl. 187. See their names.

ROMANCE OF THE MIND, metaphysics, the, xi. 269.

Romances, in four volumes, I.—IV.

CANDIDE; or, The Optimist. Vol. I.

Candide in his castle home, falls in love with Miss
Cunegund and is promptly kicked out of the place,
i. 61; his adventures among the Bulgarians, 64; he
escapes and has singular experiences, 68; finds his
tutor, Dr. Pangloss, who tells him of Cunegund's
sad fate, 71; Candide and Pangloss encounter ship-
wreck and earthquake, 76; bad luck at Lisbon, 80;
how Cunegund is restored to Candide safe and sound,
82; her story, 85.

Candide kills two men in Cunegund's apartment, 90;
flight of Candide, Cunegund, and their friend, the
old woman, 92; the old woman tells her life story,
95; certain horrors of the slave trade and famine,
100; adventures in Buenos Ayres, Cunegund's aristo-
cratic lover, 106; Candide has to fly for his life, 109;

finds Cunegund's brother in Paraguay, 113; and is
fated to kill him, 117.

Candide and his valet rescue a couple of girls persecuted by their missing-link lovers, 119; narrow es-
cape from being cooked and eaten, 123; they reach
El Dorado, 124; playing games with precious stones,
127; an extraordinary religion, 131; court life in the
land of unlimited wealth, 135; bad luck on the journey to Surinam, 138.

How negroes were maltreated in the sugar planta-
tions, 139; news of the fair Cunegund, 141; Candide
voyages to France, and meditates on brotherly love
as a Spanish ship sinks a Dutch vessel and all on
board, 148; Candide and Martin have a pleasure time
in Paris, 153; the Marchioness is gracious, 163; affect-
ing reunion with a sham Miss Cunegund, 166; Candide at last escapes out of "hell," 168.

They visit England, 168; parable of the execution
of Admiral Byng, 169; the Carnival of Venice, 170;
meets his friend the gay Pacquette and hears her
story, 173; all is not gold that glitters, 176; Seignor
Pococuranté and his happy home, 177.

His views upon the Opera, Homer, Virgil, Horace,
and Milton, 179; Candide and Martin sup with six
ex-kings, 185; to Constantinople in search of Cunegund, 190; strange discovery of Dr. Pangloss and
Cunegund's brother, supposed to have been long dead,
193; congratulations on re-appearing after being
hanged and run through, 195; perils of politeness to
pretty devotees, 198; Candide at last finds his Cunegund, no longer a beauty but willing to wed, 200.

Marriage convinces Candide that this is, perhaps, on
the whole, not quite as delightful a world as Dr.
Pangloss had led him to believe, 203; the wise old
man who chose work rather than philosophy, 205;
Candide concludes that it is best to "take care of
our garden," 208; nevertheless, he tires of his ideal
life and sets out alone to test again the best of all

converses with a serpent, 204; they wanted to sacrifice the bull and exorcise the Princess, 211; the magician's wise counsel, 217; he gives the three prophets a good dinner, 224; Jonah's fish to swallow the White Bull, 228; the serpent entertains the Princess with stories, 230; the Princess was not beheaded after all, 236; the White Bull [Nebuchadnezzar] resumes human form and marries the beautiful Princess, 239.

THE MAN OF FORTY CROWNS. National poverty, ii. 244; his disaster, 246; the geometrician explains things, 250; adventure with a Carmelite, 268; a talk with the Minister of Finance, 271; The Man of Forty Crowns marries and has an heir, 275; on paying taxes to a foreign power, 282; on proportions, 285; a quarrel over Marcus Antoninus, 293; a rascal repulsed, 296; good suppers, good talk, and good books, 300.

ROMANCES—CONTINUED. VOL III.

JEANNOT AND COLIN, iii. 5. How fortunes are made and the envious snarl at the fortunate, 6; Colin becomes a marquis, 7; what is the good of education? 9; love, marriage, and disinterested friendship, 17.

MICROMEGAS. A voyage to Saturn by a native of Sirius, iii. 20; Micromegas discusses philosophy with the Saturnian, 24; they take a trip among the rings and moons of Saturn, 29; then they visit our little Earth, 32; Micromegas the gigantic picks up a warship, 36; they are astonished that human mites can talk, 39; and shake with laughter when one of the mites professes to know all about the universe and the power behind it, 49.

THE TRAVELS OF SCARMENTADO. What he learned at Rome, iii. 51; and saw in France, and England, Holland, and Spain, 52; adventure with the Inquisition, 56; tolerance of the Turks, 57; missionaries in China, 59; adventures in India and Africa, the trivialities of sectarian fanaticism, 60.

THE HURON, or, PUPIL OF NATURE, a study of civilization. The Prior, his sister, and the young Canadian, iii. 64; of Indian blood, he speaks what he thinks and acts as he pleases, 68; he proves to be the Prior's nephew, 79; is promptly converted and baptized, 83; falls in love with his godmother, 88; beats the English single-handed and goes to court for his reward, 100; lands in the Bastille, 108; his opinions on stage plays, 119; an elopement, 126; the beautiful Miss St. Yves releases her lover, 140; her experiences of pious friends, 144; her death, 154.

THE PRINCESS OF BABYLON. Royal contest for the hand of Formosanta, iii. 164; her three lovers and their gorgeous gifts, 167; the Young Shepherd triumphs in the competition, 178; the wonderful talking bird, 182; Formosanta on her travels, 212; hears news of her chosen lover, 224; adventures in Rome and Paris, 242; discovers him in a shocking situation, but eventually forgives him, 248.

THE WORLD AS IT GOES. Ithuriel despatches Babouc to report on the Persians, iii. 266; peculiarities of war, 268; and of city ways, 270; pulpit and stage, 275; traders, clerics, and men of letters, 279; Ithuriel spares the people because they are not so wicked as their censors paint them, 288.

THE BLACK AND THE WHITE. Young Rustan adores the Princess of Cachemir, iii. 290; strange story of his travels to her country, 292; how he listens to two contradictory oracles and obeys the one which promises well but turns out ill, 293; death in the moment of victory and life is much of a nightmare, 303.

THE GOOD BRAHMIN. Does happiness result from ignorance, or from knowledge? iii. 312.

ROMANCES—CONTINUED. VOL. IV.

ANDRÉ DES TOUCHES IN SIAM. How much happier a nation would be if it could exchange its governing machine for good music, iv. 5.

.

triumph at Moscow, 142; victories of Charles XII.
of Sweden, 166; defeated by Peter the Great, battle
of Poltava, 191; conquests of Peter, 199; campaign
of the Pruth, 217; marriage of Peter and Catherine,
253; events of 1712, 263; Peter's prosperity at its
zenith, 290; he travels through Europe, 296; reception in France, 301.

Return of the Czar, xxxv. 5; proceedings against
his son, Alexis, 11; national progress after 1718,
60; trade of Russia, 66; laws and religion, 76; treaty
of Nystad, 84; conquests in Persia, 94; death of Peter
the Great and coronation of Catherine I., 108; original
documents of state, 121; appendix; climate, customs,
commerce, etc., 143; anecdotes of Peter the Great, 194.
RUYTER, MICHEL ADRIANZOON, ADMIRAL DE, 1607-1676, xxii.
162, 169.

A PHILOSOPHICAL DICTIONARY.

VOL. XIII.—CONTINUED.

RAVAILLAC—ROME.

RAVAILLAC, FRANCOIS, 1578-1610, the assassin of Henry IV.,
xiii. 44; his father confessor demonstrates that the
murderer had gone to heaven and his royal victim
to hell, 45; God takes care of His elect, 48.

REASONABLE, RIGHT. Sound thinking and plain speaking
are virtues that are liable to be punished more severely
than vices and crimes, 48; fate of the wise man who
spoke the truth to the Pope and the Sultan, 50.

RELICS, pagan worship of, 51; the trade in them, 54;
miracle at the finding of Stephen's remains, 55; drinking bouts on the tombs of saints, 57; their ghosts
dealt death among those who meddled with their
tombs, 59.

RELIGION. The wise minority may philosophize as they
please among themselves but, if you have but a village
to govern, it *must* have a religion, 61; pure worship
possible without mutilation of the person, 62.

(End of Philosophical Dictionary.)

S

" But stranger far, what few will e'er believe

> In future ages, or yourself conceive,
> The barbarous mob, whose hearts with added fire
> Those holy savages, their priests, inspire,
> Even from the carnage call upon the Lord,
> And waving high in air the reeking sword,
> Offer aloud to God the sacrifice abhorred."
> —*The Henriade*, xxxviii. 33.

St. EVREMOND, CHARLES, 1613-1703, xxiii. 128, 148; xxxviii. 301.

St. JAMES, the brother of Jesus, was Bishop of Jerusalem, first of all the bishops, xiv. 185.

St. JANUARIUS, the miraculous boiling of his blood, xiv. 17.

St. MEMIN, MADAME DE, her ghost declared she was in hell because her husband had paid the church too little for her burial, xiv. 167.

St. PETER was not the first bishop of Rome, because the first church built in that city was dedicated to St. John, known as the St. John Lateran Church today, xiv. 185.

St. PIERRE, L'ABBÉ DE, 1737-1814, xxxviii. 301.

SAINTED VAGABONDS who had no merit but ignorance, enthusiasm and filth, xiv. 30.

SAINTLY BEINGS. "Saints are men." xiv. 158.

SAITH ONE OF THEM. "Your sensible women are very fond of fools at times."
> —*The Prude*, xviii. 182.

SALADIN, 1137-1193, his first conquest, love in war, xxv. 113; a great Persian soldier, 114; his magnanimity to his defeated foe, King Guy of Lusignan, 115; his rigor in punishment, 115; his toleration of the Christian faith after his capture of Jerusalem, 116; his noble character contrasted with that of Christian tyrants, 117; Europe alarmed at his victories, 1188; Richard of England disarms Saladin, 120; who died in 1195, leaving money to be divided among the poor Mahometans, Jews, and Christians, 121.

SALIC LAW, THE, gospel authority for, xxix. 292, 297; xli. 258.

SALT OF THE EARTH.
"The friends of truth and justice are grown old
In honest poverty; above the pride
Of wealth, which they disdain."
—*Brutus*, xv. 246.

SAMSON, dramas and comedies on, xiii. 166.

SANCTA SIMPLICITAS.
"From time to time her eyelids shut would be,
Naught seeing, she believed that none could see."
—*La Pucelle*, xl. 154, 169.

SATAN given the mastery of the world by the early church, xii. 90.
—— the name is from the Persian and Job was said to have been a Persian, xxiv. 46; note, xli. 268.

SATIRE ON MAUPERTIUS, as Dr. Akakia, xxxvii 185.

SATIRICAL TREATMENT OF HIS LIBELLERS, Voltaire's Canto VI., *La Pucelle*, xl. 195-212.

SATIRIST, THE. "Indeed, Mr. Wasp, you make yourself a great many enemies."
—*The Scotch Woman*, xviii. 6.

SAURIN, JOSEPH, a scholar and free-thinking priest of universal genius, xxx. 151.

SAVAGE AND A BACHELOR OF ARTS. See DIALOGUES.

SAVONAROLA, GIROLAMO, 1452-1498, Dominican monk, who thought that a talent for preaching qualified him for governing the nation, xxvi. 200; his popularity with the people is opposed by a clever Franciscan, backed by the Pope and the Medici family, 201; the country and church split into furious parties; a challenge to try Savonarola's sanctity by the fire test is accepted, but declined in view of the burning stakes, 202; he was seized and tortured, and by virtue of an alleged confession that he was an impostor, he was strangled and burned, 202.

SAXE MARSHAL, 1696-1750, natural son of Augustus II. of Poland, xx. 119; victorious at the siege of Prague, xxxiii. 56; fighting in Bohemia and Bavaria, 88; com-

mands the French army in Flanders, 219; siege of
Tournay, battle of Fontenoy, 225.

SCALIGER, JOSEPH, his translation of the Hermes Trisme-
gistus, x. 54.

SCANDAL MONGERS. "He works himself into families to bring in misery where there is none and to
increase it where there is."
                    —*The Scotch Woman*, xviii. 17.

SCANDERBEG, the title of an Albanian, named John Cas-
triot, who tried to hew his way to the throne of the
Sultan, xxvi. 109; he recovered possession of his
father's petty sovereignty, 110.

"SCARMENTADO, THE TRAVELS OF." See ROMANCES.

SCARRON, PAUL, first husband of Madame de Maintenon,
xxiii. 183; xxxviii. 305.

SCEPTICISM OF HISTORY, THE, xxxvii. 269-280.

SCEPTRE. "Power supreme is not to be divided."
                    —*Catiline*, xvii. 248.

—— and censer, two mighty powers, xii. 271. See POPES.

SCHISM OF THE WEST, the great, xxv. 243; Pope Urban,
1378, threatened to depose a few kings; a cardinal
shook his fist in the Pope's face and said he lied;
Europe took up the quarrel, a civil and religious war
lasted forty years over the rival Popes, each of whom
pronounced the other to be Antichrist; a third Pope
was chosen over the others in 1409, John XXIII.,
who was deposed for crimes, 257.

SCHOLARSHIP IN THE MIDDLE AGES, xiv. 202.

SCHOLASTICISM in the fifteenth century, the "Summum" of
St. Thomas Aquinas, sham learning, grave foppery,
absurd fancies conveyed in unintelligible jargon, xxvi.
204.

SCHULENBERG, MARSHAL, Count of Poland, xx. 109; defeated by the Swedes, 721; letter from Voltaire to,
concerning matters in the History of Charles XII. of
Sweden, xxi. 53.

SCIENTIFIC LORE. "Knowledge, if not to prudence
joined, is vain."
                    —*The Utility of Sciences*, xxxvi. 249.

SHADOW.
>" The greatest good is ever dashed with grief;
>No bliss is pure." —*Olympia*, xv. 126.

SHAFTESBURY, LORD, 1621-1713, all is for the best, xii. 86.

SHAKESPEARE, 1564-1616. "It is much to be lamented that we find so much more barbarism than real genius in his works." xxx. 59.

—— The tragedy of Hamlet nearly on the same plan as that of the "Electra" of Sophocles; analysis of; "Shakespeare has done nothing more than turn into dialogues the romances of Claudius, Gertrude, and Hamlet, written entirely by Saxo, the grammarian, to whom the whole glory of the performance is due." [An amusing critique, in which the poetical and dramatic genius of the playwright seem to be too lofty for perception from the seat of the eighteenth century French theatre-goer; note the rendering of Hamlet's soliloquy, xxxix. 124-140.]

It seems as if nature took pleasure to unite in the head of Shakespeare all that we can imagine great and forcible, together with all that the grossest dullness could produce of everything that is most low and detestable. xxxvii. 137.

SHAM LIBERTY.
>" Our laws should with our manners change;
>That liberty thou dotest on is no more
>Than the fool's right to hurt himself."
>—*Cæsar*, xix. 132.

—— VIRTUE. "I am very virtuous, says a miserable excrement of theology." xiv. 161.

SHARING. "Happiness uncommunicated is no happiness at all." —*The Tatler*, xviii. 278.

"SHAVE With a Hired Razor, The Lord shall, and shall whistle for the flies that are in the brooks of Egypt, and for the bees that are in the land of Assyria." These performances were to celebrate the virgin birth of Immanuel, and the passage, quoted from Isaiah, "should confound the Jews and make the Christian

religion triumph, in the opinion of all our great
theologians." xiii. 20.

SHEEP OF THE FLOCK. "Am I ridiculously to ask
of others what I am to seek, or to avoid, to praise or
condemn? Must the world decide my fate? Surely
I have my reason, and that should be my guide."
                                    —*Nanine*, xviii. 97.

SHIRT, did luxury begin with the making of the first
shirt, or when it was starched and ironed? xi. 154.

SICILIAN VESPERS, THE. John de Procida, d. 1303, dis-
guised as a friar, plotted the massacre of the French
in Sicily when the bell rang for Easter Sunday vespers.
Two versions of the massacre of 1282, xxv. 169.

SILLY DISPLAY. "You love pomp and splendor, and
place grandeur and nobility in a coat of arms; I look
for it in the heart."   —*Nanine*, xviii. 96.

SILVER QUESTION, THE, in the seventeenth century; how
gold and silver, going from America to Europe, gets
swallowed up in Hindostan, never to re-appear, xxix.
141; why the natives of India have never earned
more than each day's bare subsistence, 142.

SIMON DE MONTFORT, d. 1218, the Maccabee and land
stealer, xxv. 174; his end, 177.

SIMON THE MAGICIAN. The Simon Magus with whom
St. Peter had a contest of skill. Simon not only made
things fly across the stage, but made himself wings;
he flew, but fell, vii. 113.

SIMPLE SPEECH.
        " Thou speakest the language of pure love,
        And nature; thus may lovers always speak."
                                    —*Pandora*, xvii. 297.

SIRVEN FAMILY, THE, atrocious persecution of, viii. 24,
xxxviii. 245. See TOLERATION.

SISTERHOOD.
        " Truth, ever banished from the courts of kings,
        Dwells on her lips, and all the art she knows
        Is but the generous care to serve the wretched."
                                    —*Mariamne*, xvi. 220.

SNOBBERY. "To boast of a title, if we have one, is the part of a fool, and to assume one when we have no right, that of a knave."

　　　　　　　　　　　　—The Scotch Woman, xviii. 9.

SOBERING DUTIES.
　　　　" Duties and honors which awhile
　　　To serious contemplation souls dispose."

　　　　　　　　　　　　—Olympia, xv. 165.

SOBIESKI, JOHN, 1629-1696, King of Poland, xxii. 213.

SOCIAL CHARMS.
　　　" Whose converse all mortals must equally please,
　　　With vivacity mixing an elegant ease,
　　　And a natural vein of true humor and wit."

　　　　　　　　　　　　—To M. Pallu, xxxvi. 241.

—— STATUS.　　　　　　　　　" Rank
　　　And title, objects that are envied still
　　　By all mankind, pursued with eagerness,
　　　And gained with rapture."

　　　　　　　　　　　　—Amelia, xvi. 94.

SOCIETY. "This world is nothing but a lottery of wealth, titles, dignities, rights, and privileges, bartered for without legal claim, and scattered without distinction."　　　　　　　　*—Nanine,* xviii. 113.

—— " Their heads with trifles well are filled,
　　　In trifles they are deeply skilled;
　　　And if some man, with sense endued
　　　Should in their presence be so rude
　　　To speak like one who books has read,
　　　And show he wears a learned head,
　　　With anger fired they on him fall,
　　　He's persecuted by them all."

　　　　　　　　　　　　—On Calumny, xxxvi. 91.

SOCRATES, B. C. 429-399; a chat with him in the Shades, xiii. 68.

—— THE PLAINSPEAKER. "Between you and me Socrates is in the right, but then he should not be in the right so publicly. * * * After all, what is there in poisoning a philosopher, especially when he is old and ugly?"   —*Socrates*, xvi. 307.

SODOM AND GOMORRAH. How could five towns exist near a lake of undrinkable water? The country around was asphaltic, vi. 77.

SOLDIER, A NOBLE.

"I saw him gray in arms, yet undismayed,
Dear to his friends, respected by the foe,
Firm in all states, majestic though in woe;
Expert alike in battle or retreat,
More glorious, even more awful in defeat."
—*The Henriade*, xxxviii. 28.

SOLDIERS OF FORTUNE.   "Gracious gods!
Drive from this earth those base and savage men
Who shed with joy their fellow creatures' blood."
—*Mahomet*, xvi. 57.

SOLOMON, KING, B. C. 1015-977; his wealth and family circle, xxi. 199.

SOMETIMES.

"Wouldst thou have me purchase empty honors
With infamy and shame?"   —*Mérope*, xv. 52.

SOPHOCLEAN art became enervated by love intrigues, xv. 5.

SORBONNE, THE, and the Jansenists, xxi. 141; the institution and its reverend doctors, note, xl. 54; xli. 252.

SOREL, AGNES, 1409-1450, and Charles VII. of France, note, xl. 51; xli. 253.

SOUL, THE, discussion of a dozen philosophers on a desert island, *Essays*, xxxvii. 152. See FREE WILL, SOUL, xiii. 261; GOD, SPIRIT, xxxv. 219-275; xxxvii. 152.

SOUL, THE.

"And shall its existence (like bodies) soon cease?
I know not, but I have good hope it will brave
Death, the ruins of time and the jaws of the grave;
And that an intelligent substance so pure,
The Almighty intended should always endure."
—*To M. Genonville*, xxxvi. 235.

SOUND ARGUMENTS often lead to martyrdom, xiii. 48.

—— Succession disputed, "War of 1741," xxxiii. 39.

SPARE HUMANITY.

    " Humbly the great Creator I entreat,
      This gulf with sulphur and with fire replete,
      Might on the deserts spend its raging flame;
      God my respect, my love weak mortals claim."
                  —*The Lisbon Earthquake*, xxxvi. 10.

SPARROW'S HEALTH, A; how nine Ave Marias saved its
    life but imperilled the safety of the universe, xiii. 28.

SPECULATION, WILD.

    " Above the rest appears that Scotchman famed,
      New King of France; John Law the cheat is named;
      A crown of choicest paper decks his head,
      And on its front is 'System' plainly read;
      Around him float huge bags, puffed up with wind,
      Caught at by those whose reason is quite blind;
      Priests, warriors, strumpets, think to gain ten-fold,
      And thus from each he bears away the gold."
                  —*La Pucelle*, xl. 105, 122.

—— " Public affairs are strangely carried on; stocks rise,
    the nation's rich, and I'm ruined."
             —*The Scotch Woman*, xviii. 11.

SPINOZA, BENEDICT, his philosophy examined, ix. 224; com-
    pared with Mirabaud, 76; he changed the thought,
    but not the face, of the world, xi. 131; xxxv. 243;
    xxxviii. 232.

—— "One must detest his atheism; let us not calumniate
    him in condemning him. * * * Atheism cannot
    benefit morality and may do it a good deal of harm.
    It is almost as dangerous as fanaticism." xxxviii.
    231; xxxvii. 159.

SPIRIT, soul, wind, breath, that which animates us and
    leaves us at death, xiv. 239. See SOUL.

"SPIRIT OF LAWS," criticisms of Montesquieu's, xi. 100-108;
    x. 99.

SPIRIT-RAISING, an ancient art, but the ancient witches and
    wizards never come back, xi. 163.

SPRINKLED CHRISTIANS, vi. 204.

STAGING OF DRAMAS, criticism of the French mode, *Essays,* xxxvii. 134.

STALWARTS.

> " When vulgar mortals, groveling and obscure,
> Form ill-digested schemes, and idle plans
> Of future greatness, if one slender wheel
> Is broke, it overthrows the whole machine,
> But souls like ours have naught to fear."
> —*Catiline,* xvii. 254.

STANDARDS that vary according to locality, in law, justice, weights and measures, viii. 48.

STANISLAUS, KING, father-in-law of Louis XV., xxxiii. 25.

STATESMAN, THE GOOD.

> " Fearless, and void of art,
> Never affects the pride of rank and title,
> The less he seeks for greatness,
> The more is he admired, the more revered."
> —*Sémiramis,* xvii. 151.

—— THE BAD.

> " Perish each statesman cruel and unkind
> Who reigns despotic o'er the human mind."
> —*The Henriade,* xxxviii. 23.

STATES-GENERAL assembled after the death of Henry IV., xxviii. 128.

STEALING AND DESTROYING VOLTAIRE'S WORKS, *The Age of Louis XIV.;* "the most infamous trick that ever disgraced literature," x. 87.

STENBOCK, GENERAL, of Sweden; his savage victory over the Danes, xx. 209, 282, 285.

STERCORISTS, Disputes of the, concerning what happened in a certain place, after having fulfilled a sacred duty, of which we must speak only with the most profound respect, xiv. 201.

STERNE, LAWRENCE, 1713-1768, "the second English Rabelais," vii. 238.

STIMULUS. "I want thy courage, not thy tears."
> —*Catiline,* xvii. 232.

STRING OF SHAME. "To suffer is nothing, but to be degraded is terrible." —*Nanine*, xviii. 139.

STOICS.

> " The sect he follows is a sect of fools
> Perverse and obstinate, whom nothing moves,
> Intractable and bold; they make a merit
> Of hardening minds against humanity."
> —*Cæsar*, xix. 102.

—— and Epicureans, their gods, xiii. 305; xxxv. 280.

STORIES OF NOAH, LOT AND ABRAHAM, ix. 180.

—— of Fenelon's secretary, xiv. 206; of the Jews, xxi. 193.

—— of youthful lovers forced into monastery and convent, with details of tortures inflicted on the young monk by ecclesiastical rule, as related by the victim to Voltaire, xiv. 181.

STRONG MAN, THE.

> " As firm and fearless as if honor guided
> And patriot love inspired him; ever secret
> And master of himself; no passions move,
> No rage·disturbs him; in his height of zeal
> Calm and unruffled." —*Brutus*, xv. 249.

STUARTS, THE, an unhappy and unlucky house during three centuries. James I. was murdered by his own people; James II. killed in battle; James III. killed by rebels; James IV. killed in battle; his granddaughter, Mary Stuart, imprisoned eighteen years and then beheaded; her grandson, Charles I. of England, beheaded as a traitor; his son James II. driven from three kingdoms and the legitimacy of his son disputed. This son, the Pretender, and his son, Prince Charles Edward lost their cause and were the ruin of many families of Scotland. *Age of Louis, XIV.*, xxii. 240.

STYLE AND METHOD in writing history, x. 90.

—— "He who cannot shine by thought seeks to bring himself into notice by a word." xiv. 229.

—— "In Ariosto there is no prolixity, no defect of style, no foreign ornaments; in a word he is a painter, and a

very great painter; that is the first merit of poetry."
xxxvii. 111.

—— "Cheer up, man! Put on your best looks; assume
that air of importance and self sufficiency which is
sure to conquer every heart, which baffles wit and triumphs over wisdom." —*The Prodigal*, xix. 200.

—— "How puerile is any epithet that adds nothing to the
sense!" xxxvii. 107.

SUBMERGED. "I want money, and that's the most
pressing calamity." —*The Prude*, xviii. 165.

SUBMISSIVE INCREDULITY, viii. 330.

SUCCESS. "My mother is right; address and cunning
are absolutely necessary in this world; there is no suc-
ceeding without them." —*The Tatler*, xviii. 268.

SUICIDE, strange cases, vii. 19; laws against, 29; in England, xxxix. 39.

—— "When all is lost, and not even hope remains,
To live is shameful, and to die, our duty."
—*Mérope*, xv. 56.

SUMPTUARY LAWS, luxury always condemned, but always
coveted, xi. 155.

SUN AND MOON, stopped in their daily round by Joshua,
Jupiter and Hezekiah, viii. 92.

SUPEREROGATION.
"I know to friendship Greece has temples raised,
To interest none, though interest's there adored."
—*Oylmpia*, xv. 114.

SUPERSTITION ONLY DARKNESS, morality is light, xii. 20.

—— in the tenth and eleventh centuries, xxix. 242.

—— is the most dreadful enemy of the human race, xxxvii.
230.

—— "O superstition, how thy savage power
Deprives at once the best and tenderest hearts
Of their humanity!" —*Mahomet*, xvi. 23.

SUPERSTITIONS, OLD.
"Why would ye call forth from their dark abyss
The foes of nature, to obscure the light
Of these fair regions." —*Pandora*, xvii. 294.

A PHILOSOPHICAL DICTIONARY.

VOL. XIII.—CONTINUED.

SAMOTHRACE—SYSTEM.

more than hope or fear or love, if charity does not act, xiv. 161.

THEOLOGICAL CONTROVERSY, CURE FOR. "The sudden and immense fortunes made at that time, the excess to which luxury and voluptuousness of every kind was carried, put a stop to all ecclesiastical disputes. Thus pleasure and dissipation brought about that which all the power and politics of Louis XIV. could not effect." —*Jansenism*, xxi. 173.

THERAPEUTAE, THE, vii. 132.

THIRTEENTH CENTURY, Europe in the, battle of Bouvines, xxv. 61; wars of the Popes and Kings.

—— theological science in the, xxix. 279; arts and customs, 298.

THIRTY sects of Christians in the first century, vilifying each other, xiv. 105.

THOMAS AQUINAS against conscience, vii. 237; on the soul, xiii. 314.

THORN, an eye disorder cured by kissing one of the thorns from the crown of Jesus, xxi. 152.

THOROUGH. "I never look upon things as done till they are really so."
                              —*Socrates*, xvi. 276.

THOUGHT GIVEN TO US BY GOD, x. 107, 111.

THOUGHTS ON THE PANORAMA OF HISTORY, xxx. 305.

—— on the Public Administration, xxxvii. 226.

THREE GREAT EVILS, idleness, vice, and want, can be kept off by labor, i. 206.

THREE SOULS OF ANTIQUITY, the senses, the breath, the intelligence, xiii. 266.

THRONE.   " Virtue on a throne
    Is sure the first and fairest work of heaven."
                              —*Mérope*, xv. 45.

—— OF GOD.
    " God we should search for in ourselves alone;
    If He exists the human heart's His throne."
                              —*The Law of Nature*, xxxvi. 23.

"TIMAEUS," THE, of Plato; its trinities, xii. 209.

TIMESERVERS.

"Long time thou wert thy king and country's friend;
But in the days of public discord, fate
Attached thee to another cause; perhaps
New interests now may call for new connections."
                              —*Amelia*, xvi. 109.

TIMELY WISE. "They thought they loved one another, and in two months they were parted."
                              —*Nanine*, xviii. 137.

TIME WORKS WONDERS. "We cannot give our
hearts a second time."   —*Alsire*, xvii. 41.

TIMIDITY.

"I know the consul's prudence; so he calls
His cowardice, which deeply ruminates
On future ills."   —*Catiline*, xvii. 241.

TINGLES AND TORTURES. "Love has two quivers,
one filled with darts tipped with the purest flame,
which enhances our pleasures; the other is full of
cruel arrows, that wound our hearts with quarrels,
jealousy, coldness and indifference."
                              —*Nanine*, xviii. 93.

TITHE EXACTION, clerical parasites, viii. 40.

TITLES, the more free a people are the fewer titles and
ceremonies, vii. 36.

—— of honor, significance of, xxxvii. 203.

TITLE, HEREDITARY. "Titles are of no use to posterity: the name of a man who has done great things
commands more respect than the most sounding
epithet."
                     —*Age of Louis XIV.*, xxii. 205.

TOADIES. "A crowd of parasites, who lived upon my
bounty, complimented my fine taste, my elegance, my
delicacy, borrowed my money—"

"Ay, poor devil, you did not hear them laughing at
you as they went away, making a joke of your foolish
generosity."   —*The Prodigal*, xix. 180.

TOASTS, the custom of drinking them absurd, but a genial
absurdity, viii. 168.

Toleration, A Treatise on. [*The famous protest against the cruelties perpetrated in the name of religion, based on the torture of Jean Calas and his family.* See i. 27.]

Facts of the case, iv. 118; consequences of the execution of Calas, 134; sketch of the Reformation, 137; whether toleration is dangerous, 143; Socrates and the Greeks, 161; Roman persecutions of Christians, 165; Martyrdoms and false legends, 173; toleration among the Apostles and the Jews, 202; the example set by Jesus, 235; testimonies against persecution, 246; intolerance illustrated, 249, 252, 257, 260. Is superstition serviceable? 264; virtue better than learning, 269; of universal toleration, 272; an appeal to the Deity, 277. Sequel of the Calas case, 286.

—— best weakens sectarianism, x. 45; it never was a clerical virtue, 47. See Ignorant Philosopher; Inquisition; Philosophical Dictionary; Toleration; xxxviii. 245, 254, 258, 260.

TO-MORROW. "Hope disappointed is the worst of sorrows." —*Orestes*, xvii. 102.

TOO LATE.
" When once a man is in the ground,
He hears not fame's loud trumpet sound."
—*To Madame De*......, xxxvi. 223.

Toothless prophets never listened to with the respect due to their character, xiii. 26.

Torquemada and the Inquisition, x. 221. See Inquisition.

Tournaments, died out with chivalry, about 1560, xxvi. 312.

Towns, town franchises, states-general, fourteenth century, xxvi. 61.

Trades, Origin of, xxxvi. 154; they flourished under Queen Elizabeth, xxviii. 20.

TRADE AND PROGRESS.
" The treasures of the earth and main,
With all the creatures they contain,

These, luxury and pleasures raise,
This iron age brings happy days."
—The Worldling, xxxvi. 84.

TRAGEDY, Ancient and Modern. See xix. PREFACES; HAM-
LET; xxxvii. 115; xxxix. 44.

TRAGEDY OF BROKEN HEARTS and shattered lives through
monkish vows in early youth, xiv. 181.

TRAGEDY AND COMEDY, xxxix. 122-174. xix. 235.

TRANSLATIONS, FRENCH, of the Latin poets inadequate,
Essays, xxxvii. 107.

TRANSTAMARE, HENRY DE, defeats Don Pedro, and commits
suicide, xxvi. 10.

"TRAVELS OF SCARMENTADO, THE." See ROMANCES.

TREACHEROUS MEMORY. "Falsehood in memory's
temple makes abode."
—To the Academy of Sciences, xxxvi. 260.

TREASON. "Treason is horrible in every shape."
—Brutus, xv. 276.

TRENT, COUNCIL OF, 1550, how convoked, xxi. 69; tiff between Pope Paul III. and Emperor Charles V., 70;
four years release from purgatory for all in the city,
70; some of the questions discussed, 74; murder of the
Pope's bastard son, 75; Emperor Charles proposes a
union between Catholics and Protestants, 76; death of
Pope Paul, and election of Julius III., 78; transub-
stantiation, 79; more awkward murders, 80; the Council is forgotten for ten years, but revived in 1560,
amid military and ecclesiastical display, 81; disputes
between ambassadors for precedence, 1562 and 1563,
82; the French government accepts a large bribe from
the Pope, on condition that the Huguenots are driven
from France, 84; quarrels about cups and drinking,
85; the Council tries to limit the control of the civil
power over the church; anathemas are hurled at those
who do not worship relics and deny the doctrine of
purgatory. The Council ends after extending its
sittings over twenty-one years, including interruptions,
90.

TRIAL BY ORDEAL, the earthquake entombment of Korah in his competition with Aaron, two hundred and fifty of his followers killed by lightning; and fourteen thousand seven hundred adherents otherwise destroyed, xii. 111; Aaron's rod budded; other Bible lotteries, 112; swallowing and handling fire now a stage performance, 113.

TRIMMERS. "Those
Who change with ease are either weak or wicked."
—*Sémiramis*, xvii. 179.

TRINITY, THE; the arithmetic of the Athanasian creed, vi. 20.

"TRISTRAM SHANDY" quoted and praised, vii. 238.

TRIVIALITY. "We gild and varnish cabinets, yet neglect true architecture; in short, real merit is overlooked in almost every art and science, in favor of agreeable trifles." —*Essays*, xxxvii. 123.

TRULY GOOD, THE.
"Who with his wheedling cant caressed him bland,
With air devout, and godly squeeze of hand."
—*La Pucelle*, xli. 68.

TRUMPS.
"These are your claims, and I acknowledge them; ·
But I have one that's worth them all: I love her."
—*Sémiramis*, xvii. 168.

TRUTH COMPELS AGREEMENT, error prolongs sectarianism, xiii. 185.

TRUTH-SEEKING.
"Let truth be sought, but let all passion yield;
Discussion's right, but disputation's wrong."
—*On Disputation*, viii. 134.

TSAR, the Russian word we mis-spell Czar, xxiv. 250.

TURENNE, MARSHAL, xxii. 42, 65, 85; glorious campaign and death of, 175; xxxviii. 118; note, xl. 117.

TURKS, THE, their conquests, virtues, vices, and moderation in government; the delusion that the Sultan is despotic. See AMURATH; MAHOMET II, and xxvi. 122;

their religion austere and worthy of respect, xiv. 111;
tribute to their honor in war, xx. 226.

TURKISH WOMEN, erroneous notions of their subjection,
xiv. 261.

TURN OF THE TIDE.

"We must yield submissive to our fate
If e'er we hope to change it."

—*Orestes*, xvii. 77.

TWO COMFORTERS, THE. See ROMANCES.

—— divinities, worthy to be loved for themselves, God,
and Virtue, xiv. 163.

TWO TO ONE. "He will make you an excellent husband: is not this better than a convent?"

—*Nanine*, xviii. 121.

TYRANT LOVE. "Love claims his own,
And will be heard in spite of all;
His orders are not doubtful or obscure."

—*Sémiramis*, xvii. 197.

A PHILOSOPHICAL DICTIONARY.

VOL. XIV.—CONTINUED.

TABOR—TYRANT.

TABOR, a low hill spoken of as a mountain, xiv. 42.

TALISMAN, a charm or phylactery, a time-honored superstition which flourishes as universally to-day as ever,
43.

TARTUFFE, Moliere's hypocrite, 43.

TASTE, not simply seeing and knowing a thing, but feeling and being affected by it, 44; an intellectual quality that can be cultivated, 45; the best taste is to imi-
tate nature faithfully, with energy and grace, 48; taste
is formed gradually, 51; difference between national
standards of taste, 53; true taste quickly recognizes
beauty amidst defects and defects amidst beauties, 54;
rarity of people with good taste, 56; Louis XIV. was
born with it, 57; the gifted minority ultimately correct the misjudgments of the shallower majority, 58.

TAUROBOLIUM, the sacrifice of expiation, 58.

TAX. Fee. The church gave nothing for nothing, 59; sold all its heavenly privileges according to size of the fee; prices for absolution under Pope Leo. X., 60; six drachmas for rape, five for parricide, etc., 61; sliding scale for other offenses, 62; Lenten fasting voided by payment of the church fee, 64; first night marriage rights taxed by priests and lords, 65; church secures its share of every legacy, 67; curious price list of church sanctions, 68.

TEARS, the silent language of grief, 69; our eyes a demonstration of an omnipotent creative power, 70; the true merit of the theatre is that it restores to us our unsophisticated nature, 71.

TERELAS, or Pterlaus, the man whose immortality was in a lock of his hair, which he feared to comb; how it was cut off, and what happened, 72; the Samson myth, 73.

TESTES, ecclesiastical rulings on, 74; Mosaical discrimination in selecting priests; virility an essential, 77.

THEISM, a religion diffused through all religions, 79; true that a little philosophy makes a man an atheist and much philosophy leads to the knowledge of a God, 79; theism is good sense not yet instructed by revelation, and other religions are good sense perverted by superstition, 80; it never persecutes, 81.

THEIST, is firmly persuaded of the existence of a Supreme Being, equally good and powerful, but does not presume to know how He acts, 82; to do good is his worship; to submit to God is his doctrine, 83.

THEOCRACY, in Japan, Egypt, Persia, Phœnicia, and over the Jews, 83; the Jewish republic anarchical, 86; the Papacy truly theocratical, 88.

THEODOSIUS, 346-395, the pious persecuting emperor, 88; his sentence of death by torture of those who petitioned for lighter taxation, 89; the truth about this royal "Saint," 90; the world revolves under necessity, insurmountable fatalism, 92.

THEOLOGIAN, he knows all about the unknowable, 92;

(End of Philosophical Dictionary.)

U

USAGE. "Custom hath made restraint familiar to me."
—*Zaïre*, xix. 24.

USE AND ABUSE.
" God gives to man, at once severe and kind,
Passions to raise to noble deeds the mind,
They're dangerous gifts, although 'twas Heaven
that gave;
The abuse destroys, the prudent use can save."
—*The Nature of Pleasure*, xxxvi. 244.

USURY, MORAL. "To spend money in doing good is
putting it out to the best interest."
—*The Scotch Woman*, xviii. 55.

UTILITY OF HELL TO THE CHURCH, x. 31; and of all superstitions, xiv. 19.

UTILITY OF TRADITIONS.
" Their sacred laws, for sacred they esteem
The musty rolls, which superstition taught
Their ancestors to worship. Be it so,
The error may be useful, it employs
The people, and may make them more obedient."
—*Orphan of China*, xv. 200.

UTRECHT, THE PEACE OF, xxxiii. 20.

A PHILOSOPHICAL DICTIONARY

VOL. XIV.—CONTINUED.

UNIVERSITY—USAGES.

UNIVERSITY. Origin of universities, 138; the Popes became
masters of public instruction, 139; from the fourteenth
century a doctor, on receiving his cap, had to swear
he would maintain the immaculate conception of the
Virgin Mary, 141.

USAGES. Contemptible customs do not always imply a contemptible nation, 141; each religion has its peculiar
ceremonies and symbols, which look ridiculous to those
who do not know how they originated, 142.

(End of Philosophical Dictionary.)

V

VIA MEDIA. "All excess is guilty." —*Alzire*, xvii. 44.

VICARIOUS FOLLY. "I think he is a great fool who makes himself miserable by the follies of others."
          —*The Prude*, xviii. 235.

VICE, A WISE. "He is covetous, and every covetous man is wise, it is an excellent vice for a husband."
          —*The Prodigal*, xix. 146.

—— "Vice is bewitching, temptations frequent, and example dangerous."   —*The Prude*, xviii. 200.

VICES. "Vices are tyrants of the human mind."
          —*Envy*, xxxvi. 183.

VILLAINIES of Pope Alexander VI. and Cesare Borgia, xxvi. 216.

VILLARS, MARSHAL DE, xxiii. 21; his valor and unpopularity, 22, 39; defeated at Malplaquet, 78; victorious at Denain, 94; ends the war, 104, xxxviii. 111.

VILLEROI, MARSHAL, xxiii. 8; captured by Prince Eugene, 10, 28, 40; at Ramillies, 46.

VIRGIL, viii. 252; Lucan, 254.

VIRGIN BIRTHS, ix. 153.

—— tributes to feudal lords, viii. 37.

VIRGINS, THE SEVEN, xi. 221; the eleven thousand martyred virgins buried at Cologne, xxxviii. 259.

VIRILITY REQUIRED in those who serve the altar, xiv. 77.

"VIRTUE between men is a commerce of good actions. He who has no part in this commerce must not be reckoned." xiv. 164.

—— " Fragile is man, and woman, too, my friend,
      Wherefore take heed, on virtue don't depend;
      The vase, though fair, is only formed of clay,
      'Tis easy broken; mend it, true, you may."
          —*La Pucelle*, xli. 213.

VISION OF BONES, trophies of centuries of slaughter by the faithful of the faithful and their betters, xiii. 65.

VIVIANI, geometrician, xxiii. 150.

VOITURE, his variable taste in verse, xiv. 49; his poetry compared with that of Waller, 191; his best work is over-wrought, 228.

VOLTAIRE, Francois Marie Arouet de.

Born November 21, 1694; died May 30, 1778, i. 15; imprisoned in the Bastile, 1717, where he wrote *The Henriade*, 16; pensioned by the Regent, 16; visit to England, 16; protests against the refusal of Christian burial in the case of Adrienne Lecouvreur, 16; begins *La Pucelle*, 17; *Zaïre* produced, 1733, 17; secures contract for army supplies, 17.

Marquise du Châtelet, commencement of friendly relations with, 1734, 18; and with Frederick the Great, 1736, 18, who became King of Prussia in 1740, 19; *Mahomet* produced, 1742, 19; appointed Historiographer of France, 1745, 20; gains the Pope's friendship and is elected to the Academy, 1746, 20.

Offends Madame de Pompadour and is exiled from France, 1747, 21; death of Madame du Châtelet, 1749, 21; residence in Paris, producing new plays in his private theatre, 1749, 21; visit to Frederick the Great at Sans Souci, 1750, 22; published *The Age of Louis XIV.*, and coöperated in the "Encyclopædia," 1751, 23; the satire on Maupertuis, 1752, 23; quarrel with the King and departure from Prussia, 1753, 23; arrested at Frankfort by the King's order, 24; makes his home in Geneva, naming it *"Les Délices,"* 1755, 24.

Impressive poem on "The Lisbon Earthquake," 1756, 25; *La Pucelle* offends the clergy of Geneva, hence removal to Lausanne, 25; builds private theatre at Ferney, 25; wrote the *Life of Peter the Great* at request of Elizabeth, Empress of Russia, 1758, 26; splendor and prosperity of his estate, 26.

His "Natural Religion" publicly burnt by the common hangman in Paris, 1759, 27; rumored death moved Oliver Goldsmith to write his eulogy of Voltaire [see 32], 1760, 27.

The Calas atrocity denounced in "Toleration," 1761 [see vol. iv.], 27; his heroic, persistent and triumphant efforts, during three years, result in the vindication of the injured and restoration of their property, 1765, 28;

compels justice to be done in the Sirven case, 1763-1772, 28; asserts his rights as a churchman, 1768, 28.

Turns the Ferney theatre into a watch-making factory, and established looms for silk stocking weaving, 1770, 29; the Ferney products eagerly bought in the world's best markets, 29; "The Innkeeper of Europe" invaded by distinguished visitors of every nationality and creed, 29.

Makes another theatre at Ferney, and adopts "Belle-et-Bonne," 1776, 30; his immense business enterprises and income, 1777; physical and intellectual activity at eighty-three, 30.

Last visit to Paris, after twenty-eight years' exile, 1778, 30; his royal reception by all ranks; his intercourse with Benjamin Franklin; causes a medal to be struck in honor of Washington, 31; rehearses new play, *Irène;* splendid ovation in the theatre, 31.

Death, May 30, 1778, and burial, June 1; eulogium delivered by Frederick the Great, and special services in Berlin, 31; purchase of Voltaire's library by Catherine II. of Russia, 32; grand public act of veneration on the transference of Voltaire's remains from the church of the Romilli, where they had reposed for thirteen years, to the Panthéon of France, July 10, 1791, 32.

VOLTAIRE, Tributes to, Oliver Goldsmith on, "Citizen of the World," i. 32.

—— Life Purpose of, i. 39.

—— Victor Hugo's oration at the Voltaire centenary, i. 44.

—— Characteristics. His first letter in English, xxxviii. 211.

—— Letter to a professor of history on the true method of writing it, xxxvii. 280.

—— his chemical experiments, xxxviii. 196.

—— on the making and keeping up of good roads, xiii. 148.

—— his address on his reception into the French Academy, xxxvii. 5.

—— his delight with Frederick the Great, xxxviii. 221.

VOLTAIRE, SELF-PORTRAYED.

"I have taken particular care not to depart from that simplicity so strongly recommended by the Greeks and so difficult to attain—the true mark of genius and invention."   —*Orestes*, xvii. 66.

—— "I preach simplicity to English poets, and easy numbers."   —*Preface to Zaïre*, xix. 7.

—— "The love of humankind, which always animated my heart, and which I will presume to say is my distinguishing characteristic."

—*Letter to Frederick the Great*, xxxviii. 165.

—— "I was inspired * * * by the love of mankind and the hatred of fanaticism."

—*Letter to Frederick the Great*, xvi. 6.

—— "Fate ordained that I should write."

—*To a Lady*, xxxvi. 180.

—— "I have consulted my own heart alone, which has always guided me, inspired every word, and directed every action."

—*Preface to the Orphan of China*, xv. 175.

—— "All I can boast of is that the piece is tolerably simple; a perfection, in my opinion, that is not to be despised."   —*Preface to Zaïre,* xix. 6.

—— "Readers should always distinguish between the objections which an author proposes to himself and his answers to those objections, and should not mistake what he refutes for what he adopts."
    —*Preface to Lisbon Earthquake,* xxxvi. 7.

—— "Prejudice will never allow two species of excellence to one man."   —*Preface to Catiline,* xix. 259.

VOLTAIRE, HIS REVERENCE FOR THE DIVINE.
"I say there is but one God, in his nature infinite, nor can any being partake of this infinity * * * all nature speaks one God and one father."
    —*Socrates,* xvi. 304.

—— "It is an insult on the divinity to conceive that he could possibly, in any manner whatsoever, commit with woman the crime we call adultery."
    —*Socrates,* xvi. 305.

—— "Be careful above all not to turn religion into metaphysics; its essence is morality; dispute not, but worship."   —*Socrates,* xvi. 304.

See x. 109.

VOX POPULI.
"With fears dejected, or inflamed with hope,
Still in extremes, the giddy multitude
Tumultous rove and only interest binds them."
    —*Mérope,* xv. 41.

A PHILOSOPHICAL DICTIONARY

Vol. XIV.—Continued.

VAMPIRES—VOYAGE.

VAMPIRES, corpses who went out of their graves at night to suck the blood of the living, causing consumption, 143; these flourished in middle Europe; the only vampires in Paris and London have been stock-brokers and traders who suck the blood of the people in broad

(End of Philosophical Dictionary.)

W

——   " Are wars and slaughter
    The harbingers of wisdom and of peace?"
                    —*Mahomet*, xvi. 40.

WAY OF THE WORLD. "The few * * * (are outspoken in their approval of the true and good), the rest of the world withhold their approbation for a time, but will come in at last, when the rage of party

is over, the injustice of persecution at an end, and the clouds of ignorance dispersed."
—Preface to Orestes, xvii. 67.

"WE MUST CULTIVATE OUR GARDEN," though this is the best of all possible worlds, i. 207, 240.

WEAK, THE. "One should never tell people of their danger till it is past."
—The Scotch Woman, xviii. 56.

WEAK COUNSELS.
" True courage lies in knowing how to suffer.
And not in stirring up rebellious crowds
Against their sovereign." *—Mariamne*, xvi. 262.

WEAKNESS. "The weak deceive, the powerful command." *—Mahomet*, xvi. 42.

WEALTH. "The love of money destroys more families than it supports." *—The Prodigal*, xix. 174.

WEAPONS OF WAR in the fourteenth century, xxv. 288, 314.

WEATHERVANES. "What a heap of fulsome compliments, false oaths, joyous welcomes, have I received from this whole city! but no sooner were they acquainted with my distress than every soul forsook me." *—The Prude*, xviii. 166.

WEDLOCK.
" Thou bidst Alzire give her hand to Guzman,
And at the altar promise him a heart
Which is not hers to give." *—Alzire*, xvii. 14.

WELSH, DISCOURSE ADDRESSED TO THE [Actually to the French], ridiculing their national vanity, xxxvii. 89.

WESTPHALIA, THE PEACE OF, 1648, end of the dispute between emperors and the princes of the Empire, which had lasted seven centuries, xxviii. 247.

WHIGS AND TORIES, rise of, in England, Presbyterians and Episcopals, xxiii. 91.

WHISTLING FOR FLIES, THE LORD, xiii. 20.

"WHITE BULL, THE." See ROMANCES.

"WHITE, THE BLACK AND THE." See ROMANCES.

WICKEDNESS, is it born in us? xi. 181.

WIFE, THE IDEAL. "A woman indeed, a woman submitting to every duty of life, a woman who for me has renounced the whole world, who to her faithful passion joins the most scrupulous virtue."

—*The Prude*, xviii. 192.

WIFEHOOD. "It is a wife's duty to make herself as amiable as possible, to be discreet and prudent, affable and agreeable, but as for love, it is quite another thing; my husband must deserve my heart before he can possess it." —*The Prodigal*, xix. 152.

WILLIAM THE CONQUEROR, note, xli. 124.

WILLIAM III. OF ENGLAND, battle of the Boyne, xxii. 233; character, 294.

WILLS, not legal unless a priest shared in the making, xiv. 32.

WINE IN EDEN.

"Eve, first formed by the hand divine,
Never so much as tasted wine."

—*The Worldling*, xxxvi. 85.

WISDOM. "I heed not these rash fools!"

—*Amelia*, xvi. III.

——IN SOLUTION. "I own I dread the Senate."

—*Catiline*, xvii. 266.

——much needed by poets, but few are so endowed, xii. 218; no objection to poets killing themselves, but all are not wise, 220.

WISELY AND TIMELY. "The man that drinks is never melancholy." —*The Prude*, xviii. 259.

WISE MEN. "Who consider they have fulfilled every duty when they worship God, assist man, cultivate friendships, and study philosophy."

—*Socrates*, xvi. 273.

——(or were they only kings) who came from the East to Bethlehem, stargazing, viii. 258.

WISHING. "We cannot wish for joys we never knew."

—*Zaïre*, xix. 23.

WITCHCRAFT. "The curate of Loudun was burnt at the stake by order of Cardinal Richelieu because, being a clever conjuror, he was held to be possessed by devils," xxii. 34; vi. 235; xxvi. 57; xxx. 256.

Theresa of Hungary; Elizabeth of England; Catherine II. of Russia, 71; other historical examples, 73.

—— do not reign in France, under the Salic law, because
Scripture says that lilies neither toil nor spin, and
for other reasons, xi. 65.

WOMEN'S READING. "A middling romance will serve
for two or three hours' amusement to a few women,
with whom novelty is the most essential quality in
books, as it is in everything else."
                                    —*Essays*, xxxvii. 81.

—— gift of tears, xiv. 70.

WORDS, their convenience in veiling the ignorance of the
wise, viii. 323.

"WORLD AS IT GOES, THE." See ROMANCES.

WORSHIP OF IDOLS, images of gods were not the gods,
nor is veneration of a loved portrait worship of it,
x. 127.

WORTH, INTRINSIC. "Shines the diamond with less
lustre, or is it less valuable, because found in a
desert?"   —*Nanine*, xviii. 109.

WORTHIES.   "There are exalted spirits
    Who claim respect and honor from themselves
    And not their ancestors."   —*Mahomet*, xvi. 26.

WRETCHEDNESS.
    "To fear, and to be feared; the bitter poison
    To all my happiness."   —*Orestes*, xvii. 90.

WRITERS, time of Louis XIV., biographical and critical
sketches, xxxviii. 267.

WRONG-HEADED, many ways of being, xiv. 254.

WYCLIFFE, JOHN, 1324-1387, a brave and pure reformer,
xxv. 262.

A PHILOSOPHICAL DICTIONARY.

VOL. XIV.—CONTINUED.

WALLER—WOMEN.

WALLER, EDMUND, 1605-1687, his poems liked in France,
191; the cultivation of literature by English nobility,
192.

that match, and sometimes it is the expressing only half of your thought, leaving the other half to be guessed, 222; out of place in danger and passion, when plain expressions are the fittest, 223; he who cannot shine by thought tries to attract notice by a new fangled word, 229; a man of spirit, what it means, 232; novel expression necessary to spirited speech, 232; an author wishes to show himself, when he should only show his personages, 235; Goldsmith's delicate touch, 235; wit and pretty fancies, out of place, are blemishes, 236; false wit, false style, 237; various biblical terms to describe soul; all words describing the understanding are metaphors, 240; French wit, *esprit*, 242; poetical metaphors, ridiculed by Molière, 250; how early teachings often distort the intellect, 253; the philosophy of truth-speaking and absurdity of pushing it to extremes, 254.

WOMEN, curious theories of the ancients, 255; their physical characteristics, unfitted for the work of men, 257; Montesquieu's blunder respecting the Greek word for women's love, 258; many learned women, but seldom or never are they distinguished for invention, 259; they can reign in monarchies, but have never been allowed to take part in the government of republics, 259; great Queens, Isabella of Spain, Elizabeth of England, Maria Theresa of Hungary, 260; errors respecting Mahometan subjection of women, 261; polygamy in various lands and periods, 262; stories of polyandry, 265; retort of the Mussulman to his Christian censor, 267; detailed analysis of the story.

(End of Philosophical Dictionary.)

X

XAVIER, FRANCIS, ST., 1506-1552, his gift of tongues and working divine miracles, ix. 103, 108.

A PHILOSOPHICAL DICTIONARY.

VOL. XIV.—CONTINUED.

XENOPHANES—XENOPHON.

XENOPHANES, B. C. 500, Bayle's panegyric on the devil, 269; whims of the ancient philosophers, 270.

XENOPHON, B. C. 444-359, friend of Socrates, warrior, philosopher, poet, historian, and agriculturist, 271; the retreat of the ten thousand, 272; its obscurities, 276.

(End of Philosophical Dictionary.)

Y

YOKE OF LOVE. "He who feels the yoke that is put on him will always murmur at it, and tyrannic love is a deity that I abjure." —*Nanine*, xviii. 94.

YOUTHFUL FOLLY.

" Of youth misguided, let us learn, whate'er
Their follies threaten, never to despair.":
—*The Prodigal*, xix. 233.

A PHILOSOPHICAL DICTIONARY.

VOL. XIV.—CONTINUED.

YVETOT.

YVETOT, the little town that claimed to be a kingdom, 280; story of King Clotaire, Grand Chamberlain Gautier, and Pope Agapetus, 281; some wholesale excommunications, 282; even of kings, 286.

(End of Philosophical Dictionary.)

Z

"ZADIG." See ROMANCES.

ZAÏRE, Voltaire on, xxxviii. 217.

ZAPORAVIANS, THE, the most remarkable people in the universe, *Charles XII.*, xx. 168,

A PHILOSOPHICAL DICTIONARY.

VOL. XIV.—CONTINUED.

ZEAL—ZOROASTER.

(End of Philosophical Dictionary.)

A HUMOROUS POSTSCRIPT.

CPSIA information can be obtained
at www.ICGtesting.com
Printed in the USA
LVHW020331040720
659663LV00002B/138